RANGERS
On This Day

RANGERS
On This Day

History, Facts & Figures from Every Day of the Year

PAUL SMITH

RANGERS
On This Day

History, Facts & Figures from Every Day of the Year

All statistics, facts and figures are correct as of 31st July 2012

© Paul Smith

Paul Smith has asserted his rights in accordance with the Copyright, Designs and Patents Act 1988 to be identified as the author of this work.

Published By:
Pitch Publishing (Brighton) Ltd
A2 Yeoman Gate
Yeoman Way
Durrington
BN13 3QZ

Email: info@pitchpublishing.co.uk
Web: www.pitchpublishing.co.uk

First published 2012

A catalogue record for this book is available from the British Library.

ISBN 978-1-9080513-3-2

Typesetting and origination by Pitch Publishing.
Printed in India by Replika Press Pvt. Ltd.

To Coral, Finlay, Mia and Zara

ACKNOWLEDGEMENTS

Sometimes the best things come in surprise packages and *Rangers On This Day* is one of those from an author's point of view. It was a joy to work on and a voyage of discovery, so my thanks first and foremost must go to Jane and Paul at Pitch Publishing for the opportunity to tackle an intriguing project. Gareth Davis, in editing the manuscript, and Colin MacLeod and Phil Kelly, by proof reading, also made valuable contributions. Last, but far from least, the biggest thanks of all go to Coral, Finlay, Mia and Zara for their incredible love and support.

INTRODUCTION

The recent history of Rangers Football Club has been punctuated by votes, meetings and deadlines.

Whilst each has been important in its own right, the dates that count are not necessarily those that have shaped the modern make-up of a sporting institution but rather those spanning so many pulsating decades.

The championship glory, cup victories, Old Firm triumphs, individual heroics and European memories have all gone down in history to be revered and remembered.

Rangers On This Day recounts all of the major milestones, noting occasions sure to give every loyal supporter goose-bumps. The celebrations, the goals and the reasons to be cheerful as well as offering the chance to pause and reflect on darker days which have impacted upon the Ibrox family.

But the pages that follow are about far more than simply noting the big events. Delve deep into the history of Rangers and you find some incredible quirks and intriguing pieces of trivia that sit side by side with the incredible achievements of the players who have graced the Ibrox turf through the decades.

From the opening of the social club, and its various guises in the years which followed, to the revamp of the subway station and the hoax kidnapping of a Gers favourite – there's something to stir the memories of fans young and old.

The foundations upon which the club was built are recalled, and the many characters who have had a significant impact on the life and times of Rangers. Dates, in the main, that are to be savoured, to be debated and to be enjoyed.

Paul Smith (@PaulSmithBooks)

RANGERS
On This Day

JANUARY

TUESDAY 1st JANUARY 1901

William Wilton and his team rang in the New Year in the best possible fashion as they defeated Celtic at home to put the 1900/01 championship out of reach of their Old Firm rivals. Goals from Finlay Speedie and John McPherson gave them the two points that allowed them to celebrate with three games still to play.

MONDAY 1st JANUARY 2007

A statement was issued confirming skipper Barry Ferguson had been dropped from the team by manager Paul Le Guen and that Gavin Rae would take over as captain for the following day's match at Motherwell. The relationship had begun to show cracks when the Frenchman suggested the captain's role was not as important as many might think. The decision to dump Ferguson proved to be the beginning of the end for le Guen.

SATURDAY 2nd JANUARY 1971

This was the blackest day in the long history of Rangers football club. When 66 supporters died following the collapse of barriers on Stairway 13 at Ibrox, following a 1-1 Old Firm draw in which Colin Stein had scored a dramatic late equaliser, a nation united in grief. The horror of that day resonated far beyond Glasgow, as the full extent of the disaster began to sink in. The Rangers players did what they could to console the injured during hospital visits and the families of the victims, attending every funeral, but the impact of this day would be felt forever by everyone connected with the club.

TUESDAY 2nd JANUARY 2001

The memorial to the victims of the Ibrox disaster was unveiled outside the ground on this day by club owner David Murray. The bronze statue of John Greig, listing the names of the 66 victims who died in 1971 and the 25 killed in the 1902 tragedy, was the focal point of the 30th anniversary of the tragic events. The unveiling was accompanied by a memorial service attended by around 470 relatives as well as members of the emergency services and club representatives. More than 5,000 also watched the service on big screens within the ground.

MONDAY 3rd JANUARY 1983

Motherwell 3 Rangers 0. It was a significant result in more ways than one as John Greig's struggling side was picked apart by Jock Wallace's aggressive outfit at Fir Park, hot on the heels of a New Year's Day defeat against Celtic. Described as the poorest display of the season to that point, the comprehensive defeat against the struggling Lanarkshire side was another blow to Greig's hopes of surviving in the position and also gave the Rangers directors a reminder of the fighting qualities Wallace could instil in a team. He may not have been the first choice to replace Greig, but the former Ibrox boss did enough to win a second shot at the top job.

THURSDAY 4th JANUARY 2007

David Murray announced that the club had parted company with boss Paul Le Guen by mutual consent. It left the departing manager with the dubious honour of being the shortest serving ever to grace Ibrox, lasting just seven months and taking charge of 31 games. Murray, the owner, said it had become clear replacing the manager was in the best interests of the club after a disappointing period under his guidance, punctuated by the rift with captain Barry Ferguson and unrest among supporters. The Frenchman went on to rebuild his career with Paris Saint Germain before sampling international football with Cameroon and then the Oman national team as his globetrotting adventures continued.

THURSDAY 5th JANUARY 2012

This was the controversial date set by the SFA to hear Rangers' appeal against the red card meted out to Lee McCulloch for allegedly throwing an elbow at St Mirren's Graham Carey. The appeal itself was run of the mill, but the fact the evidence would not be considered until 5th January was – because it ensured McCulloch was free to face Celtic in the Old Firm game falling before the hearing, avoiding the automatic suspension that should have followed his red card. Manager Ally McCoist was accused of playing the system, but insisted he believed his player was innocent and had every right to appeal. McCulloch eventually lost his appeal and Rangers, with the veteran in the team, lost the derby 1-0.

SATURDAY 6th JANUARY 1968

Recently appointed manager Davie White launched a broadside at the game's governing bodies, proving to be ahead of his time with an argument that too much was expected of football players in the 1960s game. White watched his side defeat Falkirk 2-0 on this day, just four days after a 2-2 draw at Celtic, but claimed the demands of the festive programme were likely to cause injury as recovery time was cut short and strength-sapping winter pitches took hold. The Scottish Football League dismissed his call for the New Year programme to be slimmed down from three games to two, with Celtic manager Jock Stein also voicing his disapproval of the idea.

SATURDAY 7th JANUARY 1899

This date was truly magical for the Rangers Football Club – it marked the end of the perfect league season, one never seen before or since. William Wilton's side of emerging stars played 18 matches in the First Division in the 1898/99 campaign and won every single one of them, blowing the competition clean out of the water in some style. Hearts put up a gallant fight, but still trailed by ten points by the time the term was complete. The final match of that 100 per cent run was away to Glasgow rivals Clyde and it ended 3-0 to the champions thanks to goals from Alex Smith, Miller and Robert Neil's penalty.

THURSDAY 8th JANUARY 1970

The Scottish Rugby Union held an emergency meeting to discuss a request from Rangers to use the Murrayfield pitch – two hours before the Scotland rugby team took to the field to face France. Ibrox manager Willie Waddell had asked permission to play a friendly against Hearts at 1pm on Saturday 10th January, with the rugby international scheduled to be played at 3pm. It came as the Rangers boss struggled to keep his side fit as the country was gripped by snow and ice. Murrayfield's pitch, protected by an electric blanket was seen as an alternative. The SRU were still considering the unusual proposition when Waddell withdrew his request, learning that his side would have the prospect of competitive action against Dundee United at Tannadice instead.

MONDAY 9th JANUARY 1967

Little did the Argentine midwives know in Henderson, Buenos Aires, that the baby boy they welcomed into the world would one day end up in the less sunny climes of Govan. Little Claudio Caniggia went on to be a World Cup winner with his country and also a medal winner with Rangers. He finalised his move to Ibrox under Dick Advocaat in May 2001, aged 34, having starred for Dundee in 2000/01 after his move from Italian side Atalanta.

SATURDAY 10th JANUARY 1903

Rangers rang in the New Year with a flurry of goals in 1903. First came the Old Firm derby, which ended 3-3, and then came a 2-2 league draw at home to St Mirren before, on 10th January, Auchterarder Thistle were dumped 7-0 at Ibrox in the first round of the Scottish Cup. Finlay Speedie scored a hat-trick, McDonald grabbed a double and Hamilton and Neilly Gibson also got in on the act.

TUESDAY 10th JANUARY 1984

John Paton was unveiled as the new chairman of the club. The Taggarts Motor Group chairman, who had made his name in the taxi trade, replaced the retiring Rae Simpson – with the former surgeon stepping down following a long stint in the chair. Simpson had replaced Matt Taylor in September 1975 following Taylor's death. Willie Waddell had retired from the board the previous month as the wind of change blew through Ibrox.

WEDNESDAY 10th JANUARY 2007

The homecoming was complete when Walter Smith was unveiled to the nation's press as the new manager of Rangers, having resigned from his post as Scotland boss. Smith, joined by new assistant manager Ally McCoist, returned for his second stint in charge and admitted the lure of another crack at managing his boyhood heroes was too strong to resist, accepting the challenging of repairing the damage done by Paul Le Guen's brief stint in charge. Scotland sat ahead of France and Italy in their Euro 2008 qualifying group at that stage but went on to miss the cut for the following summer's tournament.

WALTER SMITH RETURNED FOR A SECOND SPELL AS RANGER'S BOSS, WITH ALLY McCOIST AS HIS ASSISTANT IN JANUARY 2007

WEDNESDAY 11th JANUARY 1984

Ibrox was treated to a slice of Johann Cruyff magic as the veteran Dutch master played his part in the KLM Challenge Cup exhibition match against Rangers. Cruyff capped an impressive comeback from two down to give his side a 3-2 lead before Robert Prytz equalised with a penalty. Bobby Williamson and Ian Redford had given the hosts a 2-0 lead. It ended 3-3 and a shoot-out saw a certain Ruud Gullit make it 7-6 with the decisive kick.

MONDAY 12th JANUARY 1970

Willie Johnston breathed a huge sigh of relief after leaving SFA headquarters at Park Gardens. The Rangers livewire had appeared in front of the disciplinary committee after being ordered off for the fourth time in a year, with the latest red card coming against Clyde. He expected a heavy punishment but was handed a 21-day suspension and £50 fine, meaning he would miss just three games. Johnston had appealed against his dismissal but had that turned down by the panel.

MONDAY 13th JANUARY 2003

When Rangers touched down in Dubai the squad did not realise it would be the last time they would get the opportunity for some winter sun. Alex McLeish took his side overseas to recharge their batteries as he took full advantage of the SPL's winter break – an innovation that was scrapped after the 2002/03 season, having been in place since 1998/99. The Gers made the trip to Dubai in good company, with Bayern Munich and Juventus also basing themselves there for warm weather training.

TUESDAY 14th JANUARY 1986

Jock Wallace was renowned for his gut-wrenching training sessions and punishing schedule for his squad. But the Rangers' boss had a softer side to him too. After watching Davie Cooper's form dip in the 1985/86 season, hard on the heels of a trip to Australia with Scotland, Wallace showed his more considerate attitude when he ordered the winger to take a complete break from football to recharge his batteries. On this day, Cooper returned to training with a fresh vigour after his enforced break.

TUESDAY 15th JANUARY 2002

History shouldn't repeat itself, but for spells it looked as though it might as plucky Berwick Rangers threatened to repeat the Scottish Cup upset of their 1967 forefathers at Shielfield. The Borderers had to settle for a 0-0 draw but had the consolation of a big pay day at Ibrox six days later, when they were defeated 3-0 by the 'big' Rangers in Glasgow and came away with a cheque to match the respect they had earned with their performances.

MONDAY 16th JANUARY 1945

The London Gazette announced the completion of flying winger Ian McPherson's war honours, the official publication noting McPherson had been awarded a bar to add to his Distinguished Flying Cross. The two badges of honour reflected his incredible courage as one of the finest members of the RAF's flying squad during World War II, when he was a pilot on the earliest bombing raids over Germany. Service with the airforce interrupted McPherson's fledgling career with Rangers and after the war he went on to serve Arsenal with distinction.

SATURDAY 16th JANUARY 1932

Sammy English was the hat-trick hero as Brechin City were mauled 8-2 at Ibrox in the Scottish Cup first round. It was the start of a run that would lead to success in the competition, with 25 goals in seven ties. That tally was boosted by the Brechin victory, which included a Bob McPhail double, a brace from Jimmy Fleming and a Jimmy Marshall goal as the lower league side were dismantled with ease.

SATURDAY 17th JANUARY 1931

Non-league Armadale Thistle were on the receiving end of another Scottish Cup blitz by Rangers, who made a habit of racking up impressive scores against the minnows they faced in the early stages. More than 5,500 turned out at Armadale's home ground to welcome the big boys to town and they were treated to a show by Jimmy Fleming, with a hat-trick, as well as Bob McPhail, who scored two to join Alan Morton and Jimmy Marshall on the score-sheet in the 7-1 win.

TUESDAY 17th JANUARY 1984

It was a thrill a minute as Rangers became the inaugural winners of the Tennent Caledonian Sixes, the trial competition that spawned the long-running Tennent's Sixes. The first six-a-side tournament was at the Coasters Arena in Falkirk and the final was played in front of an enthusiastic crowd of 4,000 as Rangers came back from 4-2 down against Dundee to win 6-4. Ally Dawson and Billy Davies both scored before Bobby Williamson and Davie Cooper notched doubles. The prize was £8,000 for triumphing.

FRIDAY 18th JANUARY 1980

Eric Morley, the entertainment entrepreneur behind the Miss World competition and formerly of the Mecca Bingo empire, won planning permission to transform the former Rangers Social Club at Ibrox and open a nightclub in its place, the £150,000 Morley's Nite Spot. The premises were reported to have been leased to the businessman by Rangers rent free, in exchange for a profit share, but the club closed on 3rd May 1983 after being hit with a £70,000 rates bill that could not be met.

THURSDAY 19th JANUARY 1956

Rangers signed Alex Scott MK2. With the flying winger by the same name already making a big impact in the first team, the club brought a younger version to the club when they plundered Edina Hearts. Unlike his more illustrious namesake, the new recruit was a defensive player who had starred in the Edinburgh juvenile ranks as a right-back.

SATURDAY 20th JANUARY 1934

A stunning performance from Jimmy Fleming was the talk of football as the nine-goal hero helped Rangers to their record win. The amazing haul came in a 14-2 Scottish Cup win at Ibrox, with braces from Alex Venters and Jimmy Marshall as well as a goal from Nicholson completing the rout of the helpless Perthshire outfit. The only consolation for the visitors was that their two goals proved to be more than any other team managed to score against Bill Struth's well drilled team, who went on to win the trophy in what proved to be Fleming's final season in a Light Blue jersey.

SATURDAY 21st JANUARY 2012

Captain fantastic David Weir bid an emotional farewell to the Ibrox support. The veteran defender was not in the squad to face Aberdeen but appeared on the pitch at half-time to receive a presentation from chairman Craig Whyte and Andy Kerr of the Rangers Supporters Assembly. Weir received an ovation for his services in five trophy-laden years, picking up eight winners' medals in that time. He had been signed by Walter Smith in January 2007 in what many viewed as a stop-gap deal, but Weir defied his advancing years to play 231 games in a blue jersey. He had opted to leave the club having fallen out of the first team picture.

SATURDAY 22nd JANUARY 1898

It was a cup of plenty for Rangers in the 1897/98 campaign, firing 12 goals past Cartvale in the second round of the Scottish Cup on 22nd January – just a fortnight after scoring eight without reply against Polton Vale. Neither of the opposition sides was in the top flight of the Scottish League at that stage and the gulf in class was there for all to see.

MONDAY 23rd JANUARY 1956

Touring side San Lorenzo, from Argentina, turned out under the Ibrox floodlights as they brought a touch of South American flair to Govan as part of their British expedition. More than 30,000 turned out for the game and were treated to an intriguing exhibition to warm the hearts on a freezing cold night, with the Gers winning 4-3 thanks to goals from Bert Kichenbrand, Sammy Baird and a Johnny Hubbard double.

WEDNESDAY 24th JANUARY 1973

The return to European competition after the triumph in Barcelona ended in disappointment on this day when Ajax defeated Rangers 3-2 in Amsterdam in the second leg of the European Super Cup Final. Alex MacDonald, who scored in both matches, and Quinton Young were both on target but it was not enough to knock the Dutch masters off their stride. European Cup champions Ajax had won 3-1 at Ibrox eight days earlier and emerged with a 6-3 aggregate win to lift the silverware.

SATURDAY 25th JANUARY 1964

East of Scotland outfit Duns travelled from the Borders through to Ibrox on a winter's afternoon to face the mighty Rangers in the Scottish Cup second round, having played Celtic 13 years earlier in the national competition. There was to be no fairytale for the underdogs, who were beaten 9-0 as Jimmy Millar bagged four goals and Ralph Brand claimed a hat-trick to add to goals from George McLean and Willie Henderson. Within 11 years the non-league outfit had folded after losing their home ground, disappearing from the football landscape forever.

FRIDAY 26th JANUARY 2002

Dick Advocaat, director of football at Ibrox, was named as manager of the Netherlands as he prepared to combine club duties with those as boss of his home country. The Rangers talent spotter insisted he was able to do both roles as he returned to a job he had held previously, having led the Oranje to the World Cup finals in America in 1994.

TUESDAY 26th JANUARY 1966

Manager Scot Symon was furious as three of his top team stars were kidnapped outside Ibrox. Police were not involved, however, with a group of students from the Scottish Physiotherapy Hospital admitting responsibility for the stunt. The hoax was part of the fun of Charities Week, although Symon did not see the funny side. He argued that the trio of Eric Caldow, Willie Mathieson and Roger Hynd could have caught colds after being waylaid on their walk back from the Albion training ground to Ibrox. The anger of the prank did not prevent the students from carrying out a planned fundraising tricycle race at Ibrox just days later.

SATURDAY 26th JANUARY 1974

The highs and lows of knock-out football were experienced early in 1974. First Jock Wallace's side blitzed Queen's Park 8-0 at Ibrox in a third round tie that featured hat-tricks from Derek Parlane and Tommy McLean, with Ally Scott and Eric Morris also scoring. Then, three weeks later, they were brought crashing back to earth with a 3-0 defeat at home to Dundee in the next round.

WEDNESDAY 26th JANUARY 1977

It was announced that honorary president John Lawrence had died at his home near Strathblane. Lawrence was 82 and remained a popular figure at Ibrox. Having been appointed chairman in 1963 he presided over the success in the European Cup Winners' Cup in Barcelona in 1972, and was responsible for the appointment of Jock Wallace as manager as well as the earlier recruitment of Willie Waddell. Lawrence, from Govanhill, had built his company John Lawrence (Glasgow) into one of Scotland's biggest building firms and in turn developed the wealth and stature to hold the most powerful club position in the national game.

SATURDAY 27th JANUARY 1900

The Scottish Cup club record was equalled as Ayrshire outfit Maybole travelled through to Ibrox on second round duty – only to be met by a less than welcoming barrage, the Gers hitting 12 without reply to sail into the next round. Robert Hamilton scored four, Wilkie claimed a hat-trick while there were singles from Alex Smith, Robertson, Hyslop, Neil and Gibson.

SATURDAY 27th JANUARY 1996

Highland League hopefuls Keith tackled Rangers in a Scottish Cup third round tie moved from their Kynoch Park ground to Pittodrie Stadium to allow more people to attend and more than 15,000 saw Walter Smith's side blitz the underdogs with a ten-goal blast, although the hosts did at least grab a consolation to make the final score 10-1. Ian Ferguson and Alex Cleland both scored hat-tricks while Charlie Miller, Alexei Mikhailachenko, David Robertson and Gordon Durie, from the penalty spot, were also on target.

SATURDAY 28th JANUARY 1967

It was a dark, dark day as Rangers were humbled by Berwick Rangers. It was Scottish Cup day and the Ibrox side travelled to Shielfield Park full of confidence and expectation. In the end, Scot Symon's side simply could find no way through the plucky Borderers rearguard and when the minnows snatched an unexpected goal there was no way back. It proved to be the beginning of the end for the strike pair of Jim Forrest and George McLean.

GORDON DURIE WAS ON TARGET AS RANGERS HIT TEN PAST HIGHLAND LEAGUE KEITH IN JANUARY 1996

MONDAY 29th JANUARY 1990

The legend returned, with John Greig walking back through the front door of Ibrox as an employee of the club once again. When he ended his long association with the club by resigning from the manager's job, Greig could not have anticipated he would return within six years. He was invited back by David Murray, who had handed him a public relations role which involved not only dealing with the media but also acting as a liaison between the board and supporters. The role developed with the appointment of Dick Advocaat, with Greig's knowledge of the Scottish game proving invaluable to the continental coach and his experience providing the Dutchman with a sounding board for his ideas for moving the club forward.

TUESDAY 30th JANUARY 1968

An unlikely hero was born in Edinburgh. Scott Nisbet, who grew up in the capital city and came through the ranks at the renowned Salvesen Boys Club, was plucked from the east by Rangers and given his big break during the glory days of the late 1980s and early 1990s. It was on the European stage that Nisbet made his most memorable contribution - with his incredible goal against Club Brugge in the inaugural Champions League campaign, sealing a 2-1 victory. It was vital in keeping the hopes of a place in the final alive. On a mud bath of an Ibrox pitch, his dipping and swerving shot from distance bounced over the stranded Belgian keeper to send the crowd into raptures.

TUESDAY 31st JANUARY 2012

Prize-asset Nikica Jelavic was sold to Everton in a £5.5m deal, leaving manager Ally McCoist with little hope of signing a replacement before the January transfer window closed. It proved to be the last piece of business the club would do before going into administration, bringing in revenue that should have helped the ailing club battle on. The Croatian striker had become a hero at Ibrox with his displays following his £4m purchase in August 2010 and proved to be the most saleable player during a fraught period for the business. Jelavic went on to light up the English game with his displays in the opening months of his Everton career.

RANGERS
On This Day

FEBRUARY

THURSDAY 1st FEBRUARY 2001

Daniel Prodan's contract expired, ending one of the more bizarre episodes in Ibrox's life. Signed for £2.2m from by Dick Advocaat in 1998, the Romanian defender arrived with what was thought to be a minor knee injury. The same injury kept him sidelined for the duration of his stay and he never kicked a ball in anger for the first team. Although he attempted to bounce back during a loan spell with Rocar Bucharest, two years after leaving Rangers he was forced to concede defeat and retire through injury.

WEDNESDAY 2nd FEBRUARY 2005

Tense, nervous, close-run affairs. All of the best cup semi-finals follow that script but every now and again one comes along that breaks the mould and the League Cup contest with Dundee United in 2005 did exactly that. The Arabs were blown away by an irresistible Rangers at Hampden, with Alex McLeish watching his side hammer United 7-1 to reach the final. Nacho Novo and Steven Thompson both grabbed doubles while Dado Prso, Thomas Buffel and Fernando Ricksen were also in on the scoring act.

TUESDAY 3rd FEBRUARY 1981

John Greig resigned from the Scottish Managers' and Coaches Association, despite attempts by chairman Dave McParland to persuade him to reverse his decision. The gesture by the Rangers boss was shrouded in mystery, with no confirmation given to the association of the reason for breaking away from the organisation – although speculation suggested a row with Ayr United counterpart Willie McLean about the leaking of Rangers' interest in defender Steve Nicol was at the root of the rumpus.

SATURDAY 4th FEBRUARY 1967

February proved to be a good month for Alex Willoughby. On this day he kicked off the month with a hat-trick at home to Hearts in a 5-1 canter and just four days later he claimed his second match ball inside a week when he bagged a treble in a matching 5-1 victory at Clyde. Another goal, this time in a 2-1 win away to Kilmarnock, in his next outing made it seven from three outings for the sharp shooter.

TUESDAY 5th FEBRUARY 1980

The Dundee board of directors met to consider a £200,000 bid by Rangers manager John Greig for Dens Park striker Ian Redford. The Dark Blues made their Ibrox counterparts wait 24 hours to be informed of their decision, and when they did it was not good news. The offer was rejected, with Greig claiming there would be no improved figure tabled. The record-breaking deal did eventually go through, with a fee of £210,000 struck between the sides.

MONDAY 6th FEBRUARY 1984

He was not a big-money signing or an extrovert superstar, but the player who signed on this day was worth his weight in gold to Rangers. Stuart Munro, recruited by Jock Wallace for the princely sum of £15,000 in 1984 from Alloa Athletic, went on to become a dependable and important member of Graeme Souness' squad and spent seven years plying his trade at Ibrox, patrolling the left flank with aplomb. Munro was snapped up by Blackburn Rovers in 1991, with the club making a £335,000 profit on the veteran when he switched south.

MONDAY 7th FEBRUARY 2005

Walter Smith and Ally McCoist linked up on the training pitch for the first time as a coaching team, with McCoist attending his first Scotland squad gathering after accepting Smith's invitation to join the national team staff alongside former Celtic boss Tommy Burns. That gathering in Manchester marked the launch of a pairing that would see the duo move from Scotland back to Rangers as manager and assistant and then pave the way for McCoist to take over as Ibrox boss in his own right.

SATURDAY 7th FEBRUARY 1970

Forfar Athletic presented a potential banana skin on a winter's day in Angus but they found themselves up against a professional and well organised Rangers team who produced a seven goal blast without conceding against the Loons. Skipper John Greig led by example with a rare brace while Alex MacDonald, Colin Stein, Andy Penman, Sandy Jardine and Kai Johansen, from the penalty spot, also netted in the Scottish Cup second-round tie.

WEDNESDAY 8th FEBRUARY 2012

Daniel Cousin was revealed as the man Ally McCoist had targeted to replace Nikica Jelavic following the striker's January departure for Everton. The 35-year-old free agent's recruitment hinted at the financial strife within Ibrox, arriving back in Glasgow almost four years after last kicking a ball during his first stint in Light Blue. The Gabon forward arrived promising to fire Rangers back into the Champions League – little realising that within days his new employers would enter administration. He left without playing a game.

THURSDAY 9th FEBRUARY 1989

The attention to detail paid by Graeme Souness by everything that fell under his umbrella as manager was demonstrated on this day when young defender Tom Cowan joined from Clyde. Cowan was no more than a squad man during his time with the club, but Souness put the same care into recruiting him as he did with any of his £1m stars. Souness had watched the youngster in action personally on several occasions before clinching the deal.

TUESDAY 10th FEBRUARY 1948

A crowd of more than 60,000 turned out in Lisbon to watch the famous Rangers Football Club in action as Benfica rolled out the red carpet. The visitors recorded a 3-0 victory in the exhibition match, with Willie Thornton opening the scoring after 35 minutes against the run of play. Jimmy Duncason scored two in the last six minutes to give the score a more flattering appearance than the performance had merited, according to reports from Portugal.

SATURDAY 11th FEBRUARY 1950

Cowdenbeath were full of hope when they ventured across from Fife to Govan to tackle Rangers in the Scottish Cup second round at Ibrox, having come within an ace of dumping Bill Struth's side out of the League Cup earlier in 1949/50 when they were beaten 5-4 on aggregate having won the first leg in Glasgow 3-1. That hope was soon swept aside as a ruthless Rangers performance - including doubles from McCulloch, Williamson and Johnson as well as goals from Paton and Rutherford – led to an 8-0 margin.

FINANCIAL WOES MEANT ALLY McCOIST STRUGGLED TO REPLACE NIKICA JELAVIC IN JANUARY 2012

MONDAY 12th FEBRUARY 1973

Rangers called a meeting of Scottish clubs to outline bold proposals for modernisation of the game, spearheaded by general manager Willie Waddell. Twenty teams were represented as Waddell made a raft of suggestions for improving attendances and increasing entertainment. They included a new £1,000 prize for the country's leading scorer and a controversial suggestion that 0-0 draws should not be rewarded with a point. While welcomed by some representatives, it was accepted there would be too many hurdles to overcome to make the more radical proposals a reality.

WEDNESDAY 13th FEBRUARY 1985

Dynamo Moscow tackled Rangers in a repeat of the 1972 European Cup Winners' Cup Final and once again the Scottish team came out on top. A bigger crowd had made the trip to Barcelona than turned out for this friendly version, with less than 12,000 inside Ibrox for the visit of the Russians. Skipper Craig Paterson won the match with a headed goal.

SUNDAY 14th FEBRUARY 2010

Fans staged a demonstration against the Lloyds banking group during a match against Hibs at Ibrox. Supporters waved banners before the game and at half-time to express their anger at the bank's role in the running of the club, an issue first highlighted by manager Walter Smith in 2009. The Ibrox crowd called for answers from Lloyds and demanded the role and responsibilities of Donald Muir, the bank's representative on the Rangers board, be clarified.

TUESDAY 14th FEBRUARY 2012

Duff and Phelps were appointed administrators, just a day after owner Craig Whyte had filed papers stating his intention to go down that route as HMRC and other creditors began to close in. The move into administration brought with it a ten-point SPL penalty and effectively ended the hopes of retaining the championship, ultimately the least of the worries of supporters as the extent of the club's financial plight began to sink in. Whyte was bullish to begin with, but as the administrators delved deeper into the club's affairs it became apparent that there would be no quick fix.

SATURDAY 15th FEBRUARY 1958

Lower-league club Forfar were on the receiving end of the full force of Rangers when the two sides met in the Scottish Cup second round at Station Park. The tie ended 9-1 as Max Murray hit a hat-trick and Ralph Brand and Billy Simpson both notched doubles in addition to goals from Johnny Hubbard and Ian McColl. More than 8,000 had crammed into the Angus ground and were treated to an impressive display by the visitors.

MONDAY 16th FEBRUARY 1998

Dick Advocaat was confirmed as the man David Murray had chosen to replace Walter Smith when he stood down at the end of 1997/98, after a long and exhaustive search. The PSV Eindhoven boss came with a glowing reputation and had been favourite to land the coveted post. He was only announced as the new man after the details had been thrashed out over a number of weeks, with PSV understandably keen to hold on to their leader but failing in attempts to rebuff the Scottish suitors as the lure of chasing the Champions League dream proved too strong.

SATURDAY 16th FEBRUARY 1946

The curtain fell on the Southern League, with the final fixture pairing champions Rangers with mid-table Hearts. The Jambos won 2-0 at Tynecastle, but by then their opponents had long since clinched the title in a league introduced to fill the void created by the abandonment of the First Division for the duration of World War II. The competition was contested six times and in those six years the trophy was brought back to Ibrox six times as Rangers dominated.

SATURDAY 17th FEBRUARY 1894

The Scottish Cup was brought to Ibrox for the first time as the fledgling Rangers team defeated Old Firm rivals Celtic 3-1 at Hampden Park in front of 17,000 – becoming kings of Glasgow as well as Scotland, having already got the better of Clyde and Queen's Park along the way. The final was won with goals from H McCreadie, Barker and McPherson to begin a long relationship between the Gers and the trophy.

SATURDAY 18th FEBRUARY 1989

There was no mercy from Graeme Souness and his team as they welcomed Stranraer to Ibrox for a Scottish Cup fourth-round tie, having been taken to a replay by lower league opposition in the shape of Raith Rovers in the previous round and been on the brink of crashing out in a major upset. There was no question of a weakened team being fielded against lower league Stranraer, with the Stair Park side hammered 8-0 by a star-studded team. Kevin Drinkell, John Brown and Ally McCoist all bagged doubles to add to the goals scored by Ian Ferguson and Mark Walters on a day on which the Ibrox crowd got full value for money from their heroes.

SATURDAY 19th FEBRUARY 1887

Rangers waved farewell to Kinning Park and did so in style as they defeated Old Westminsters 5-1 in the quarter-finals of the FA Cup to mark the last competitive game at the site. A crowd of 6,000 had turned out for the final appearance at the ground and found a team on song as the English visitors proved no match for their goal hungry hosts and gave the old ground a fitting send-off. The club had moved to Kinning Park in 1876, taking over from Clydesdale Cricket Club following its move to Titwood. On 26th February the send-off was complete when a challenge match between the Moderns and the Ancients took place, with the Ancients drawing players from the club's early beginnings at Fleshers Haugh.

FRIDAY 20th FEBRUARY 1987

It was a time for experiments as Rangers entertained French side Bordeaux, quarter-finalists in the European Cup Winners' Cup by that point of the season and going well in domestic competition, for a challenge match. The trial of Friday night football tempted close to 30,000 out on a winter's evening while on the pitch there was another pilot scheme in operation as player-manager Graeme Souness tried himself out as a sweeper. Both experiments could be deemed a success, with the new look Rangers side, featuring Ally McCoist and Dave McPherson in unfamiliar midfield roles, defeating their continental opponents 3-2 with goals from Robert Fleck, Neil Woods and Souness.

ON THEIR WAY TO WINNING THE 1989 SCOTTISH CUP, GRAEME SOUNESS LED RANGERS TO AN 8-0 WIN OVER STRANRAER AT IBROX,

WEDNESDAY 21st FEBRUARY 1962

Replays are, by their nature, close encounters. Not this time, however. After drawing 2-2 at Pittodrie the Dons travelled to face Rangers full of optimism as they bid to cause an upset. Instead the north-east side was blown away by Scot Symon's rampant Gers, who claimed a 5-1 win to cruise through to the quarter-finals thanks to a Jimmy Millar double and goals from Ian McMillan, Davy Wilson and Ralph Brand.

TUESDAY 22nd FEBRUARY 2011

It was the realisation of a dream for Ally McCoist as he was confirmed to succeed Walter Smith as manager of Rangers. McCoist was tasked with taking over when Smith departed in May that year, not fully realising the turmoil that lay ahead. Kenny McDowell would step up from his coaching role to take the assistant manager's role vacated by McCoist in the reshuffle of the Ibrox pack, with the succession plan Smith had put in place followed through by David Murray in the final throes of his ownership of the club.

SUNDAY 23rd FEBRUARY 1975

There was one in and one out for Rangers as Willie Ormond assembled his latest Scotland Under-23 squad for a match against Wales in Swansea. Established club star Derek Johnstone dropped out due to a knee injury, with less prominent Ibrox team-mate Ian McDougall gaining promotion to join the young Scots. The midfielder, a product of Pollok juniors, was in his second season as part of Jock Wallace's first team squad. He moved on to Dundee two years later and also turned out for Berwick Rangers and Albion Rovers.

WEDNESDAY 24th FEBRUARY 1999

The Old Firm broke new ground when they announced the two clubs were locked in talks over a joint shirt sponsorship deal. Rangers and Celtic had both sported the CR Smith logo on their kits in the 1980s, but that was as the result of separate negotiations. In 1999 they joined forces to lever the best possible financial result from the talks they could, eventually agreeing a £13m four-year contract with American cable TV operator NTL.

MONDAY 25th FEBRUARY 1980

John Greig and his team touched down in Dubai for a whistlestop tour of the United Arab Emirates. They tackled Al-Nasr, winning 2-1 with goals from Derek Johnstone and Gordon Smith, before moving to Kuwait two days later to face Al-Arabi and recording a 3-1 win through Alex MacDonald, Iain Redford and Davie Cooper. Each match attracted more than 10,000 spectators, proving the club's global reach. The same season had seen Rangers travel to Canada for a series of matches in the Red Leaf Cup.

TUESDAY 26th FEBRUARY 1985

Former Rangers and Scotland goalkeeper Stewart Kennedy was awarded a testimonial by Forfar Athletic and the highlight of the programme took place at Station Park when a Gers team travelled north to tackle the Loons in a challenge match. The game ended in an honourable draw after Ally McCoist's double had given the Gers fans in the Angus crowd something to shout about.

FRIDAY 27th FEBRUARY 1998

Gordon Durie was released from the Southern General Hospital after three days of treatment. The striker had suffered a sickening head knock during a 1-1 draw at Kilmarnock on 24th February, colliding with Gary Holt before apparently recovering to play on. Five minutes later Durie collapsed to the Rugby Park turf and lay motionless as medics tended to him. He was rushed to hospital and continued to suffer headaches during his stay, with doctors insisting he would be out of action for at least a month as he recovered from suffering serious concussion.

THURSDAY 28th FEBRUARY 2002

Ian Durrant embarked on a coaching career that would eventually bring him home to Ibrox when he took his first session as Kilmarnock's new first team coach on this day. Durrant, who had been winding down his playing career with the Rugby Park club, was a surprise appointment to new manager Jim Jefferies' staff. Durrant remained with Killie until 2005, when he was recruited by Rangers to train the Murray Park youngsters before stepping up to take on first team duties.

WEDNESDAY 29th FEBRUARY 2012

This leap day was a memorable one for Dunfermline players and staff for all the wrong reasons. The events of 14th February for Rangers had a knock-on effect and The Pars were left without their full February wages because of a cash flow problem for the club, who were waiting for £85,000 from Rangers for ticket sales for the 11th February match at East End Park. This was understandably a blow to the Fife club who were already cutting costs earlier in the season by closing the North Stand at East End Park to supporters to reduce police and stewarding costs to save money to fund undersoil heating at the ground.

RANGERS
On This Day

MARCH

FRIDAY 1st MARCH 1996

Rangers were said to be trailing German striking legend Karl Heinze Reidle in the spring of 1996. Instead, Walter Smith secured Danish forward Erik Bo Andersen from Aalborg for £1.5m. The towering Scandinavian arrived with a glowing reputation, but struggled to repay manager Smith's faith in his ability and he returned to his homeland with OB in 1997. The Dane's best contribution was a match-winning double in an Old Firm encounter in 1997, replacing Ally McCoist and bagging the decisive goals in a 3-1 victory.

THURSDAY 2nd MARCH 1989

Alan Montgomery was unveiled as the new chief executive. He moved from Scottish Television with an impressive cv and a brief from new owner David Murray to spearhead a new commercial era at Ibrox. Early in his tenure, Murray recognised the need to exploit sponsorship opportunities and outside revenue streams to support his ambitions.

FRIDAY 3rd MARCH 1989

England international Mel Sterland became the first recruit of the David Murray era. The £750,000 acquisition from Sheffield Wednesday was seen as a solid capture who could boost the push for the championship at a vital stage in the season, even if he wasn't the type of glamorous signing that the club was becoming renowned for. Manager Graeme Souness stressed the new boy would need time to adapt to the pace of the Scottish game as he unveiled the latest new face. He was sold to Leeds United for £650,000 in June 1989.

THURSDAY 4th MARCH 1982

Plans for Sandy Jardine's well deserved testimonial match were unveiled. It was confirmed that Southampton, managed by Lawrie McMenemy and with Kevin Keegan as their star attraction, had agreed to provide the opposition for the Ibrox event on 9th May. The long serving defender's day in the sun attracted more than 20,000, who saw Gordon Dalziel score the only goal of the game. Rangers repaid the favour by travelling to the south coast for Saints stalwart George Horsfall's testimonial the following week, when they lost 4-2.

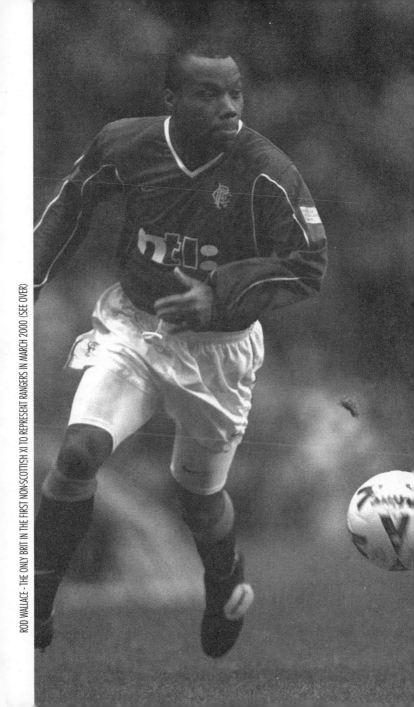

ROD WALLACE - THE ONLY BRIT IN THE FIRST NON-SCOTTISH XI TO REPRESENT RANGERS IN MARCH 2000 (SEE OVER)

SATURDAY 4th MARCH 2000

History was made as, for the first time ever, a Rangers team was sent out without a single Scotsman in its number. St Johnstone provided the opposition at Ibrox and the result did not favour the cosmopolitan Gers as they settled for a 0-0 draw. German goalkeeper Stefan Klos was behind a defence marshalled by Italian star Lorenzo Amoruso alongside Australia's Tony Vidmar, Dutchman Arthur Numan and American skipper Claudio Reyna. With another Dutchman, superstar in the making Giovanni Van Bronckhorst, anchoring the midfield and the Russian wing wonder Andrei Kanchelskis on one flank, the Germanic abilities of Jorg Albertz and Turkish talents of Tugay Kerimoglu behind English striker Rod Wallace and Chilean forward Seb Rozental.

MONDAY 5th MARCH 2012

This was due to be the day administrators Duff and Phelps announced a cull of the playing staff at Ibrox to cut costs and keep the club alive. The anticipated job losses did not materialise, however, and instead it was announced the financial troubleshooters were considering an alternative plan put forward by players in a bid to protect the roles of playing and administrative staff. After intense negotiation, it was announced on 9th March that the package of measures had been accepted, including 75 per cent wage cuts for the highest paid players, and that redundancies would not be necessary. The compromise did come with concessions, with players reported to have been able to have new clauses inserted in the renegotiated deals allowing them to move on for reduced fees if they chose to.

MONDAY 6th MARCH 1989

Borders minnows Gala Fairydean welcomed a capacity crowd of 5,000 as Rangers arrived to play in a match that saw the host side's new floodlights unveiled. Gary McSwegan hadn't read the script, scoring a double to sit alongside John Morrow's goal and give the visitors a 3-2 win. The installation of lights was part of Gala's drive to prepare themselves to bid for a place in the Scottish Football League, eventually finishing third behind Caley Thistle and Ross County when a vote was taken in 1994 and, to date, not succeeding in realising their dream of joining the senior ranks.

WEDNESDAY 7th MARCH 1956

The first ever Scottish league match played under floodlights took place – but it was Rangers who dazzled at Ibrox as the charge towards the 1955/56 championship gathered pace, They sent out a message to the chasing pack with an emphatic 8-0 victory against a Queen of the South team firmly ensconced in the top half of the First Division table. Billy Simpson, with two goals, and Alex Scott were on target against the Doonhamers but the real hero was Bert Kitchenbrand, who bagged a five-goal haul during an incredible run of form that saw him score ten goals in March alone. The South African notched 29 goals in 35 games during his short career with the club, an imposing total for an imposing man nicknamed The Rhino due to his bulky frame.

WEDNESDAY 8th MARCH 1961

Doubts over the future of the Albion as the club's training ground were eradicated as Glasgow Corporation backed down from its plan to slap a compulsory purchase order on the piece of land. Rangers had bought the former greyhound complex from the Glasgow Albion Racing Company when it had fallen into liquidation but the corporation wanted the land for housing. On this day the warring paries agreed to a compromise, with the football club told it could retain eight acres for car parking and training purposes if it released three acres for housing. The club had been using the Albion for decades prior to purchasing it.

WEDNESDAY 8th MARCH 2006

Rangers announced a ten-year agreement with retailer JJB Sports which would see the firm become sole stockists of club merchandise and replica kits, with an £18m upfront payment and annual royalties of £3m promised to the club in return for the exclusivity. Chairman David Murray said the money would be used to reduce debt and invest in the squad, but it did mark the end of an era as the Rangers Shop chain would close as part of the deal and the 200 jobs at the business were put at risk. Instead, JJB installed Rangers concessions in each of its Scottish stores to tap into the demand for anything with an Ibrox link.

SATURDAY 9th MARCH 1996

Scottish football's newest club played host to Rangers for the first time as Inverness Caledonian Thistle rolled out the welcome mat for Walter Smith and his side for a Scottish Cup quarter-final that was shifted to Tannadice to enable more than 11,000 to enjoy the occasion. The venue didn't prove lucky for the north side, still finding their feet after being formed through the merger of Highland League teams Inverness Caledonian and Inverness Thistle. They fell to a Paul Gascoigne double and own goal from Brian Thomson as the eventual winners booked their place in the last four.

SUNDAY 10th MARCH 1985

A double-header against the Iraq national side was completed in Baghdad. It ended in a 4-1 defeat, with Robert Prytz scoring the consolation goal, just two days after Eric Ferguson had scored in a 1-1 draw to open the Middle East tour. A 2-1 win against Kuwait in neighbouring Jordan rounded off the far flung adventure for Jock Wallace and his team.

WEDNESDAY 11th MARCH 1964

There was some small consolation for Willie Henderson after the Scotland star suffered a sickening injury in a 1-1 draw against Aberdeen at Pittodrie. Henderson was stretchered off after just 22 minutes with what appeared to be a broken ankle, but was later diagnosed with ligament damage. It proved to be a costly evening for the visitors, who also had Jim Forrest added to the casualty list during a bruising encounter with the Dons.

SATURDAY 12th MARCH 1949

Rangers completed the club's first ever domestic treble in 1948/49 and the trophy trail began on 12th March with the League Cup Final against Second Division opponents Raith Rovers. Bill Struth's team were huge favourites for the trophy and lived up to their billing with a composed 2-0 victory against the Kirkcaldy side courtesy of goals from Torry Gillick and Willie Paton. It would prove to be the first of three trophies claimed within the space of seven glorious weeks as the campaign drew to a dramatic climax.

MONDAY 13th MARCH 1972

Willie Henderson met with manager Willie Waddell to attempt to broker a peace deal. The winger had walked out on the club six weeks earlier after a disagreement with the boss but returned for talks aimed at restoring him to the fray. The outcome was a one-month suspension from first team games, coupled with the order of double training sessions each day in an attempt to return the Scotland star to full fitness after his absences. Henderson left soon after and missed out on the European Cup Winners' Cup Final just two months later.

FRIDAY 14th MARCH 1975

After a long delay, relatives of the victims of the Ibrox disaster were told the obstacles to them receiving compensation for their tragic losses had been moved out of the way. Insurers Norwich Union, under pressure from director Willie Waddell and Rangers, confirmed that they would not challenge the claims, paving the way for the £500,000 settlement to progress. The level of awards would vary depending on the family circumstances of the victim, while those seriously injured were also expected to be compensated.

WEDNESDAY 15th MARCH 1967

Another true Blue was born on this day, with Ian Ferguson making his arrival. It was with St Mirren rather than Rangers that he made his name but, after joining the Graeme Souness revolution in 1988, he soon showed his true colours with combative midfield performances and a thunderbolt shot during 12 years in the team. He went on to play for Dunfermline before playing and coaching in Australia.

SATURDAY 16th MARCH 1912

It took a twist of fortune to hand Rangers the title, despite the fact they had been beaten 2-1 at Dens Park by Dundee. While the blue half of Glasgow toiled on Tayside, the green and white section was struggling too as they tackled Partick Thistle at Firhill. Celtic were held to a 1-1 draw by the Jags and that left them unable to close the gap on a Rangers side who still had four games to play and went on to win the title by four points.

MONDAY 16th MARCH 1998

Bob Brannan was unveiled as the new chief executive of Rangers by David Murray. The 41-year-old was due to join up at Ibrox in June that year after agreeing to leave his post at William Grant & Sons Distillers to take on the challenge. His responsibilities would include all business and commercial aspects of Rangers, life and the new recruit said he was excited by the global reach of the club.

SUNDAY 16th MARCH 2003

The first leg of the memorable 2002/03 treble was completed in fine style with an Old Firm victory at Hampden in the League Cup Final. Goals from Claudio Caniggia and Peter Lovenkrands, an Argentine and a Dane in a team which featured sole Scot Barry Ferguson, looked to have put Alex McLeish's side on easy street before the break but a Henrik Larsson goal in the 57th minute ensured a dramatic conclusion. Neil Lennon was sent off late in the game before John Hartson put a last-minute penalty wide of the target to ensure a 2-1 victory for the Light Blues.

SUNDAY 16th MARCH 2008

The League Cup was won in the most dramatic fashion as Rangers and Dundee United fought out a 2-2 draw at Hampden Park. Kris Boyd twice equalised after the Arabs had moved ahead and when it went to penalties it was the men in blue who held their nerve to run out 3-2 winners in the shoot-out to shatter the hopes of the Tannadice team as they attempted to repeat their Scottish Cup Final triumph over the Gers in 1994.

SATURDAY 17th MARCH 1962

This date should be forever etched in the memory of Davie Wilson as the classy Scotland winger produced a stunning performance against shellshocked Falkirk at Brockville.Wilson scored six of the goals for Rangers as they galloped to a 7-1 victory against the Bairns, with Alex Scott chipping in with the other goal. The hosts recovered in time to avoid relegation – but did drop defender Jimmy Milne the following week after his torrid time trying to keep the rampant Wilson at bay.

TUESDAY 17th MARCH 1964

Rangers were in court – but the club had not been involved in a misdemeanour. Instead, officials had their application for a licence to promote football pools granted at Glasgow Magistrates Court and were able to embark on a fundraising drive that pumped millions into the club's coffers over several decades, having been instigated by director David Hope during a period of rapid commercial expansion at the club. Other initiatives included licensing fees for the use of the club crest.

SUNDAY 17th MARCH 2002

Alex McLeish won his first trophy as Rangers manager in some style as his new charges swept First Division challengers Ayr United aside in the League Cup Final of 2001/02. A double from talismanic Argentine star Claudio Caniggia as well as a Barry Ferguson penalty and that rarest of things, a goal from record signing Tore Andre Flo, gave McLeish and his men a 4-0 win at a packed Hampden Park. The hard work had been done in the semi-final when Celtic were defeated 2-1 to pave the way for the Ayr showdown.

SATURDAY 18th MARCH 1978

The first leg of the 1977/78 treble was claimed when Celtic were beaten 2-1 at Hampden in the League Cup Final. Davie Cooper and Gordon Smith did the damage for Jock Wallace's side during a season in which the Parkhead side struggled to make any impact, eventually finishing fifth and 19 points off the championship pace set by the Light Blues. A stunning 6-1 win against Aberdeen in the group stages of the competition, helped by a hat-trick from Smith, had set the ball rolling.

MONDAY 19th MARCH 2012

Duff and Phelps were officially confirmed as Rangers' administrators after a bizarre legal twist. Although appointed on 14th February, it was subsequently revealed that there had been a hitch in the process and the firm did not have the necessary authority to serve in that role. That was resolved at the Court of Session in Edinburgh, where a judge passed a retrospective order appointing them from the initial date.

SATURDAY 20th MARCH 1897

Twenty-three goals in five ties proved exactly why Rangers had their name engraved on the Scottish Cup in 1897. A 4-2 win over Partick, 3-0 victory against Hibs and 4-0 canter against Dundee was followed by a 7-2 rout against Morton in the semi-final and convincing 5-1 triumph against lower league opponents Dumbarton in the final. J Miller's double and goals from Hyslop, McPherson and Alex Smith brought the cup back to Govan.

SUNDAY 20th MARCH 2005

Mid-table Motherwell were the team standing between Rangers and the first trophy of 2004/05. The Steelmen melted away in the face of a rampant Gers side, with Greek defender Sotirios Kyrgiakos the unlikely hero with two goals in a 5-1 win in the League Cup Final at Hampden. Maurice Ross, Fernando Ricksen and Nacho Novo were also on target, with David Partridge grabbing Well's only goal as Alex McLeish and his men were left to celebrate their comprehensive triumph.

SUNDAY 20th MARCH 2011

The League Cup was on the line as Rangers and Celtic went toe to toe at Hampden. When Steve Davis had his opener cancelled out by Joe Ledley in the first half, the game raced to full-time all square. Nikica Jelavic proved to be the hero in extra time when his 98th-minute goal clinched the trophy on an afternoon on which Celtic's pain was compounded by a red card for Emilio Izaguirre as the red, white and blue ribbons were being tied to the silverware.

WEDNESDAY 21st MARCH 1990

The Albion training ground was sold after an extraordinary general meeting at the King's Theatre. There was drama to fit the venue as around 300 shareholders grilled directors on the deal – which would see the land sold to one of chairman David Murray's companies for £2m. After heated debate a vote of roughly 2-1 approved the deal, with the money to be used to cut the club's debt. No details of Murray BS Ltd's plans for the land were available at the time.

NIKICA JELAVIC CLINCHES THE SCOTTISH LEAGUE CUP, WITH THE WINNING GOAL AGAINST RIVALS CELTIC IN MARCH 2011

WEDNESDAY 21st MARCH 2001

The family section at Ibrox was launched as the club targeted a younger audience in a bid to boost interest. A strict stewarding regime was offered, with fans warned that swearing and other forms of verbal abuse would not be tolerated in the Broomloan stand. The family section was due to open in time for the 2001/02 season, catering for demand identified in surveys of supporters.

SUNDAY 21st MARCH 2010

St Mirren were the opposition at Hampden as Rangers attempted to regain the League Cup. The Buddies put up a spirited fight but ultimately were undone by the dogged determination of Kenny Miller, who scored in the last six minutes to give his side a 1-0 victory and exemplify the never-say-die spirit ingrained in Walter Smith's squad. Rangers had been reduced to ten men when Kevin Thomson was sent off eight minutes after the break.

WEDNESDAY 22nd MARCH 1967

It is hard to imagine a European quarter-final being decided on a coin toss in the modern era, with the multi-million pound consequences of every result – but that's exactly what happened on this day. The flip fell in Rangers' favour, booking them a place in the last four in the season in which they ran all the way to the final, while Real Zaragoza were left licking their wounds. The Spaniards had won 2-0 on their home patch but that was only enough for a 2-2 aggregate draw after Dave Smith and Alex Willoughby's goals at Ibrox had given the Gers a 2-0 lead.

WEDNESDAY 22nd MARCH 1972

The quarter-finals of the European Cup Winners' Cup paired Willie Waddell's side with the Italians of Torino. The second leg on 22nd March was a dramatic affair at Ibrox as Alex MacDonald proved to be the match winner with the only goal of a tense and hard fought contest, earning his side a place in the last four after a 1-1 draw in Turin a fortnight earlier. Willie Johnston was on target in the first leg.

WEDNESDAY 23rd MARCH 1988

England legend Trevor Francis was released by Rangers after his short stint in Scotland. The striker, who had featured sporadically for the Light Blues after arriving from Italian football, was set to link up with Jim Smith at Queen's Park Rangers. Smith had been his boss at Birmingham City and was keen to be reunited with the veteran striker, who was reported to have been earning £1,000 per game at Ibrox.

TUESDAY 24th MARCH 1998

Paul Gascoigne checked in at training for the last time as a Rangers player. He bid farewell to his Ibrox team-mates and the management as the finishing touches were put to the deal that would take him to Middlesbrough, managed by Bryan Robson. The £3m transfer ensured the bulk of the cash spent on the England star had been recouped after three eventful years north of the border. Gascoigne went on to play for Everton and Burnley as well as managing Boston United.

FRIDAY 24th MARCH 1989

There was a first for Rangers as reserve player Gordon Mackay received a £4,000 bursary to study sports medicine at the London Hospital. He was no ordinary squad member, but in fact was Dr Mackay. The medic was on a year's sabbatical after graduating and spent it working at Ibrox, training with the Rangers stars and playing a handful of reserve games during his stint which also saw him work closely with the club's own medical team. Mackay did have a football pedigree, having been on the books of St Mirren and Kilmarnock prior to a change in career direction.

SATURDAY 25th MARCH 1876

Moses McNeil, one of the founders of Rangers Football Club, became the first of the team's players to be capped by Scotland when he ran out against Wales at Hamilton Crescent in Glasgow. He helped the team to a 4-0 victory, but had to wait another four years for his second and last appearance in the colours of his country. McNeil featured against England in 1880 and played his part in a 5-4 victory.

SUNDAY 25th MARCH 1984

Ally McCoist savoured that winning feeling for the first time as he stole the show in the League Cup Final against Celtic at Hampden. The new recruit stunned the opposition with a hat-trick to secure a 3-2 win and lift the gloom just eight days after hopes of a cup double had been shattered by a Scottish Cup quarter-final exit to Dundee. With group stages still in operation in the League Cup, the final was the 11th game of the competition for Rangers.

SATURDAY 26th MARCH 1898

The changed face of the game is well illustrated by the run to the Scottish Cup Final in 1898. To reach the showdown with Kilmarnock, Rangers overcame long since forgotten names Polton Vale and Cartvale in the early rounds. The more familiar Killie were still aspiring to reach the First Division when they ran out at Hampden in front of a modest 14,000 crowd in the competition's infancy and were beaten 2-0 by the favourites as Smith and Hamilton scored the decisive goals to retain the trophy.

WEDNESDAY 27th MARCH 1996

Scotland had a new captain as Ally McCoist pulled on the armband for the first and only time. The honour was bestowed upon the Rangers legend for a friendly against Australia at Hampden and he marked the occasion with a 55th-minute goal that proved to be the winner for Craig Brown's side. McCoist, a decade after making his debut in dark blue, was replaced by Pat Nevin in the 80th minute, allowing him to soak up an ovation from an appreciative Glasgow crowd.

SATURDAY 27th MARCH 1948

The biggest crowd ever to watch Rangers in action filed into Hampden Park on this day. There were 143,570 inside the national stadium as Willie Thornton scored the only goal of the game allowing the Ibrox men to defeat Hibs in the semi-final of the 1947/48 Scottish Cup. The final against Morton, eventually won after a replay, attracted around 10,000 fewer supporters than the showdown with a team of legendary Hibs players who went on to become champions of Scotland that term.

WEDNESDAY 28th MARCH 1956

The novelty of floodlights was still a major draw in the 1950s, with a series of exhibition matches played to make use of the facility at Ibrox. Yugoslavian outfit Dinamo Zagreb were among the overseas teams to visit during that era and rolled in to town to play, treating a crowd of 45,000 to a 3-3 draw as Billy Simpson, Derek Grierson and Max Murray scored for the hosts.

SATURDAY 29th MARCH 1902

Victory over a Dundee side languishing just one place off the foot of the First Division table was what was required to clinch the championship for Rangers in 1901/02. The Gers duly delivered, with a 3-1 triumph putting them two points clear of Celtic when the final points tally was totted up. Scorers on the day were Hamilton, A Smith and Speedie as a crowd of 13,000 watched the Gers defend their league crown.

SATURDAY 29th MARCH 1930

It was four-in-a-row as Rangers defeated Clyde 3-0 at Ibrox to put themselves out of sight of First Division challengers Motherwell and Aberdeen with five games to spare in the 1929/30 season. Jimmy Marshall scored twice, one from the penalty spot, while Tommy Muirhead was also on target for Bill Struth's side. The league winners went on to lose three of the remaining five fixtures but still crossed the line five points clear of runners-up Motherwell.

SATURDAY 29th MARCH 1975

It had been a decade since the First Division trophy had sat in the Ibrox trophy room, a period in which Celtic had dominated the league. It was left to striking hero Colin Stein to end the Parkhead side's stranglehold in a season in which he had been brought back to the club from Coventry. The forward's headed goal in a 1-1 draw at Easter Road on 29th March carned the point that ensured the crown was Govan bound, with the Hibees the closest challengers that term. Stein's goal sparked incredible scenes of celebration in Leith, with Rangers fans making up the bulk of the 38,585 crowd.

WEDNESDAY 29th MARCH 1995

Scottish football was left numb as it was confirmed Davie Cooper had died, with the decision taken to withdraw the life support keeping him alive at Glasgow's Southern General Hospital. The Rangers legend collapsed a week earlier while filming a coaching video at Broadwood Stadium in Cumbernauld, struck down by a brain haemorrhage. More than 9,000 people lined the streets to pay their respects to the wing wizard, who had long since departed Rangers by the time of his death but who had left a lasting impression. Cooper had moved on to Motherwell in 1989 and gone on to win a whole new set of admirers among the Fir Park faithful.

THURSDAY 30th MARCH 1989

David Murray revealed ambitious plans to redevelop Ibrox. His £10m blueprint was designed to increase capacity to 52,000 with a new tier on the Main Stand. Additional executive boxes were also in the pipeline and already snapped up by eager businesses and individuals as demand for places inside the ground outstripped supply. Murray revealed his plans to fund the major work with the launch of the Rangers Bond, allowing supporters to purchase 'their' seat for life while pumping cash into the club's coffers to meet the high costs of the scheme.

THURSDAY 30th MARCH 2000

Dave King won a place as a non-executive director of Rangers – in exchange for pumping £20m into the club. The exiled Glaswegian, living in South Africa, was said to be a lifelong Rangers fan. His contribution was to be used to reduce the debt, invest in new players and to help support the Murray Park complex and the youth policy.

SATURDAY 31st MARCH 1979

John Greig won his first trophy as Rangers manager as his team defeated Alex Ferguson's Aberdeen at Hampden. Greig was tasked with leading the club through a period of transition but it was the old guard who came good with Alex MacDonald and Colin Jackson scoring the goals that ensured the rookie manager got his hands on the first piece of silverware available in 1978/79.

RANGERS
On This Day

APRIL

SUNDAY 1st APRIL 1979

The headlines were no April fool: "Wallace for Barcelona". Speculation mounted that former Gers boss Jock Wallace was destined for the Nou Camp as the Spanish giants searched for a new man to lead them to success. Reports broke claiming Wallace, in his first season in England with Leicester City after leaving Ibrox the previous summer, was next on their list as they prepared for a £5m investment in their squad. The move did not come to fruition but Wallace did eventually land up working in Spain with Seville.

TUESDAY 2nd APRIL 1974

Two club legends were brought together on the Ibrox pitch as former captain George Young stepped forward to present a silver salver to current skipper John Greig in recognition of him scoring the 10,000th competitive Rangers goal. The strike had come against Clyde days earlier, when Derek Johnstone also notched the 6,000th league goal. Both received presentations before the 3-0 league victory over Dunfermline and the celebration was saved by substitute Graham Fyfe, who scored a late double to add to Derek Parlane's earlier penalty.

FRIDAY 3rd APRIL 1987

The Ibrox Main Stand was awarded B-listed status by the Scottish Development Department. The announcement ensured that the Secretary of State of Scotland would have to grant permission for any alterations to the Edmiston Drive building. The experts behind the decision noted the stand's red brick facade, ashlar detailing, wood panelling and stained glass as features of particular note. Several other nearby sites gained A-listed status at the same time, including the Govan Graving Docks and the Govan Shipbuilders' office.

SATURDAY 4th APRIL 1964

Two first half goals against Dundee United won the 1963/64 league crown for Scot Symon's team, with two games left to play in the First Division. A bullet shot from Ralph Brand, after a trademark Willie Henderson run, and a George McLean effort put the hosts on easy street in front of a jubilant Ibrox crowd. Kilmarnock had been the closest challengers but were six points adrift by the time the final ball had been kicked.

SATURDAY 5th APRIL 1924

David Meiklejohn's penalty and Andy Cunningham's goal made it 2-1 to Rangers against Hibs at Ibrox, but the result carried more significance than normal. It gave Bill Struth the two points he needed to ensure chasing side Airdrie's challenge was ended. The rivalry with the Diamonds was a common theme during the 1920s, with the Broomfield side finding themselves the perennial bridesmaids as they finished second to Rangers in 1923, 1924 and then again in 1925.

SATURDAY 5th APRIL 1947

The Scottish League Cup was introduced for the 1946/47 season as football returned to normality after the Second World War. The new competition included a group section and Rangers emerged with six wins from games against St Mirren, Queen's Park and Morton before squeezing past Dundee United over two legs in the quarter-final and Hibs in the semis. That led to a showdown with Aberdeen at Hampden in the final and a double from Jimmy Duncanson as well as goals from Torry Gillick and Billy Williamson gave Rangers a 4-0 win and ensured the club was the first to have its name etched on the new cup.

SATURDAY 6th APRIL 1929

Jock Buchanan earned a piece of Scottish football history that he would rather not have had when he became the first player to be sent off in a Scottish Cup Final. His team were on their way to a 2-0 defeat against Kilmarnock when frustrations spilled over and Buchanan was red carded for ungentlemanly conduct, having apparently sworn at the referee during the Hampden showdown with the Rugby Park side.

WEDNESDAY 7th APRIL 1993

A place in the Champions League final slipped agonisingly away from Walter Smith and his brave side in the dramatic setting of Marseille. Although Ian Durrant's goal earned a valuable point against the French champions, victory was required to help with progress from the group stages. A 0-0 draw against CSKA Moscow two weeks later ended the campaign, with Rangers unbeaten in six ties but short of what was required to progress.

SATURDAY 8th APRIL 2000

Scottish Cup semi-final day proved to be a walk in the park, Hampden Park, for Dick Advocaat and his team. Poor Ayr United were the cannon fodder for a rampant Rangers side, hammered out of sight by a ruthless opposition. A Billy Dodds hat-trick, Seb Rozental's double and goals from Andrei Kanchelskis and Rod Wallace made it 7-0 to the SPL leaders. The treble from Dodds was made all the more remarkable by the fact he was only introduced as a half-time substitute.

WEDNESDAY 9th APRIL 1986

The speculation and rumour came to an end as Graeme Souness was confirmed as the new player-manager of Rangers. The 34-year-old Scotland midfielder had accepted the invitation to take charge at Ibrox, but would remain with Italian club Sampdoria until the end of the 1985/86 season to help their bid to stave off relegation, having led them to the Italian Cup the previous year.

SATURDAY 10th APRIL 1937

Champions Rangers wrapped up their home fixtures in the First Division with a 1-0 win over Albion Rovers in the penultimate match of the season courtesy of a Bob McPhail penalty. Bill Struth's side had strolled to the league title, ending up with a seven point lead over runners-up Aberdeen even after being beaten at Clyde in the last game of the term. The penalty was McPhail's 25th goal of the season but he was beaten to the top scorer's badge by Alex Smith, who scored against Clyde to make it 31 for the term.

WEDNESDAY 10th APRIL 2002

The popular orange change kit was launched. It came after large sections of Rangers support had donned Netherlands kits, a nod towards manager Dick Advocaat and his colony of Dutch stars. The club decided to take advantage of demand with the tangerine kit, which was part of a launch of three new strips that would be manufactured and sold by the club, under the Diadora brand, to provide a new revenue stream and cut out the middle man of a kit supplier.

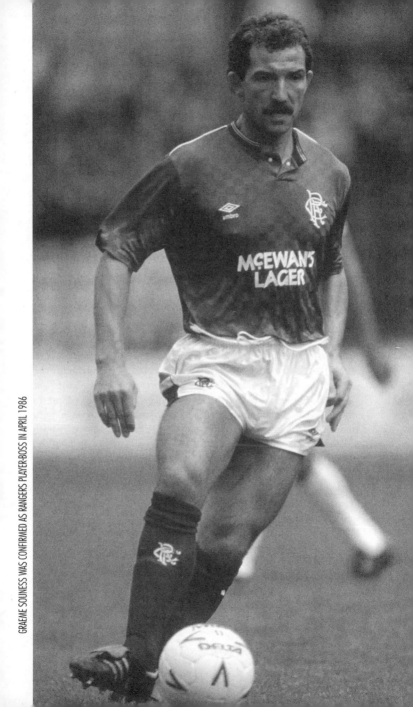

WEDNESDAY 11th APRIL 2012

The SPL announced plans that would lead to Rangers starting the following two seasons with ten-point deductions in the event of the club being liquidated and re-forming as a new company. New proposals to increase the penalty for entering administration from ten points to 15 points were also floated. Both ideas would have to be ratified by SPL member clubs, a decision none was keen to take while Rangers remained for sale.

SATURDAY 12th APRIL 1947

The title was all but won as Rangers entertained Hamilton at Ibrox on the last day of the First Division season, the first after the war. It would have taken defeat and a dramatic turnaround in goal difference to allow challengers Hibs to overtake the Gers, but that didn't happen. Instead Accies were thumped 4-1 as Billy Williamson grabbed a double, Jimmy Parlane scored and Jimmy Duncanson also hit the back of the net to get the party started.

SATURDAY 13th APRIL 1918

The First Division title went right to the final furlong in 1917/18 when Rangers managed to get their noses ahead of Celtic and take first prize. Clyde, second from bottom, were the team they had to get past along the way and like true thoroughbreds they dug deep to do just that. Goals from Sandy Archibald and James Bowie were enough for a 2-1 win and, having gone into the day in second place, they were able to creep up on the inside of the Parkhead team by virtue of the Celtic's failure to do better than draw 1-1 with Motherwell.

SATURDAY 13th APRIL 1935

It was three in a row as Aberdeen were defeated 3-1 at Pittodrie and Rangers clinched the First Division prize, stretching a lead that challengers Celtic could not match. Alex Smith, Bob McPhail and Torry Gillick scored the decisive goals in what proved to be the last win of the season. The next three games brought a draw against Albion Rovers and defeats against Hamilton and Queen's Park, although the big prize had already been won.

SATURDAY 14th APRIL 1928

The wait to bring the Scottish Cup back to Ibrox was finally ended. The competition had been re-introduced in 1920 after a six-year absence and proved to be full of frustration for William Wilton and his successor Bill Struth, with two final appearances in the seven years prior to 1928 and two defeats. Celtic were the opposition for the turning point and the Old Firm derby brought the best out of Struth's men, who trounced their biggest rivals 4-0 to lift the trophy as Sandy Archibald's double, Davie Meiklejohn's penalty and Bob McPhail's goal destroyed the Hoops.

SATURDAY 14th APRIL 2001

Scottish football was in mourning as Jim Baxter's death was announced. The former Rangers and Scotland star passed away after suffering from cancer, one of several health struggles he endured. His funeral at Glasgow Cathedral attracted the great and good of the Scottish game and many other famous faces.

WEDNESDAY 15th APRIL 1953

Airdrie travelled to Ibrox needing to win to help save their First Division status. Rangers needed to win to keep their championship dream in tact. The result? Rangers 8, Airdrie 2. It was no contest as Grierson chipped in with four goals and Prentice, Paton, George Young's penalty and a Diamonds own goal gave the hosts an impressive margin at the business end of the season. Bill Struth's team took five points from the next three games and won the title from Hibs on goal difference – boosted by the earlier victory against the Broomfield side.

TUESDAY 15th APRIL 1986

Walter Smith became a Rangers employee as he departed Dundee United's coaching staff and accepted the invitation from Graeme Souness to become assistant manager at Ibrox. Smith, right hand man to Jim McLean at Tannadice and also to Alex Ferguson in the Scotland setup, arrived as the old coaching team of Alex Totten, John Haggart and Stan Anderson were shown the door. With Souness seeing out his playing career in Italy, Smith took temporary charge for the closing games of 1985/86.

WEDNESDAY 16th APRIL 1930

The Scottish Cup became the first piece of silverware collected in the double winning season of 1929/30 as Partick Thistle were defeated 2-1 at Hampden. Goals from Jimmy Marshall and Tully Craig undid the Jags in a replay. The first game, four days earlier, ended without a goal but the favourites came good in the rematch – having already defeated the Firhill side twice in the league prior to their Scottish Cup showdown.

SUNDAY 16th APRIL 1967

This was the day that Scotland humbled World Cup winners England in *that* game, as Rangers star Jim Baxter taunted the Auld Enemy with his ball juggling on the Wembley turf. Baxter's cocky display came in a 3-2 victory over England, a side he had scored a double against in a 2-1 win in 1963 at Wembley. He played 34 times for his country, having made his debut in November 1960 just months after embarking on his career with Rangers. Those appearances brought three goals.

SUNDAY 16th APRIL 1978

Ibrox was packed to capacity as more than 65,000 supporters turned out to honour captain John Greig in his testimonial against Scotland. Fittingly the star attraction scored two of the goals as his Rangers team won 5-0 to cap a memorable occasion and give him a tangible reward for his 17 years in the Ibrox top team, having made his debut back in 1961. Within months he would swap playing for managing as he succeeded Jock Wallace in the hot seat, opting to bring the curtain down on his playing commitments as he threw himself into his new role.

WEDNESDAY 16th APRIL 1980

The Ibrox station opened its gates as the modernised Glasgow Underground system was launched. Known as Copland Road Station from the time the subway opened in 1896, the station had been closed in 1977 as part of the extensive revamp of the network but returned to normal service to become part and parcel of matchday life for home and away supporters attending Rangers games. It was one of four stations renamed as part of the modernisation.

TUESDAY 16th APRIL 1991

Graeme Souness quit Rangers to accept the challenge of reviving the fortunes of his beloved Liverpool. He departed Ibrox as his team vied with Aberdeen for the Premier Division championship and with words of caution from his friend and chairman David Murray ringing in his ears. Murray had suggested Souness would regret it in the long run, and was proved correct as his reign on Merseyside proved frustrating as he departed just three years later with only a solitary FA Cup triumph to show for his efforts.

SATURDAY 17th APRIL 1909

The Scottish Cup Final replay of 1909 should have been a day of celebration for one half of the Old Firm but instead it ended in disappointment for both as the match, and the competition, was abandoned after rioting broke out among the 60,000 crowd at Hampden. The game was poised at 1-1 at that stage, with Jimmy Gordon scoring for the Gers, a week after the two sides had been level pegging at 2-2 in the initial tie.

SATURDAY 18th APRIL 1936

It was a Glasgow derby of a different kind in the 1936 Scottish Cup Final as Rangers took on city rivals Third Lanark at Hampden. Just five days earlier the Light Blues had made the short trip to Cathkin Park on league duty and beaten their hosts 3-1, so form suggested the cup would be heading for Ibrox. That was exactly the way it turned out as Bob McPhail grabbed the only goal of the game to deny Thirds a cup win.

WEDNESDAY 18th APRIL 1956

Reigning champions Aberdeen travelled to Ibrox aiming to prevent Rangers from taking their crown, but the Dons failed to deliver. Rangers won by a single goal, scored by Alex Scott, but in reality they cantered to the victory which ensured the league flag fluttered over Govan rather than Pittodrie. The Gers, lauded as deserving champions by all who had watched them that term, failed to win any of their last three games but still emerged with a six-point winning margin.

SATURDAY 18th APRIL 1959

One of the most remarkable afternoons in Scottish league football saw an incredible set of results with an amazing list of consequences. Aberdeen won 2-1 at Ibrox, beating a Rangers team who needed to win to be sure of earning the First Division title, and in doing so climbed out of the relegation zone in dramatic style. Meanwhile, Celtic set about defeating championship challengers Hearts – to hand the title to Old Firm rivals Rangers.

FRIDAY 19th APRIL 1912

A goalless draw against Dundee at Dens Park edged Rangers five points ahead of Celtic with four points for the Parkhead men to play for, securing a third consecutive flag with a week to spare. A victory the following week at home to Falkirk completed the campaign and gave the Ibrox side a four point winning margin at the end of a season in which Reid, with 22 goals, was the standout performer.

WEDNESDAY 19th APRIL 1972

One of the biggest games ever played at Ibrox saw Rangers defeat favourites Bayern Munich 2-0 in emphatic style. With ground packed to the rafters with more than 80,000 supporters, Sandy Jardine's wonder strike and young Derek Parlane's goalscoring heroics sent the Gers fans into raptures. The foundations had been laid in Germany two weeks earlier when Bayern had been held to a 1-1 draw in Munich, with two impressive defensive performances by a team growing in confidence with every passing round ensuring the place in the European Cup Winners' Cup Final belonged to the Scottish team.

WEDNESDAY 20th APRIL 1911

The final home game of the 1910/11 season confirmed Rangers' place as champions of the land for the first time in nine years as they defeated Third Lanark 3-1 with goals from Willie Reid, Alex Bennett and Alex Smith to consign Aberdeen to the runners-up berth. The Dons had gone through the season unbeaten at home but it was not enough to get the better of a determined Gers side, who finished four points clear of the Pittodrie side despite losing in each of their encounters with them.

WEDNESDAY 20th APRIL 1932

It took two attempts, but they got there in the end. After drawing 1-1 with Kilmarnock on 16th April, when Bob McPhail was on target, they returned to Hampden four days later and finished the job with a 3-1 victory against the Rugby Park men. McPhail was again a scorer and was joined by Jimmy Fleming and Sammy English – who had notched his ninth cup goal in seven appearances, having claimed hat-tricks against Brechin City and Raith Rovers in the early rounds.

SATURDAY 21st APRIL 1928

The First Division was clinched in spectacular style as Kilmarnock were brushed aside 5-1 at Ibrox in the game that ensured challengers Celtic and Motherwell could not close the gap at the top of the table. Jimmy Fleming's hat-trick and a brace from Andy Cunningham secured the prize. It was the eighth time Bill Struth's team had hit five or more in league games that season, scoring 109 goals in 38 fixtures as the goals flowed thick and fast home and away.

SATURDAY 20th APRIL 1935

Bill Struth developed something of a stranglehold over the Scottish Cup in the 1930s and that continued in 1935 when he led his team against an in-form Hamilton side. The Accies had been among the pack chasing champions-elect Rangers in the First Division, eventually finishing fourth but only four points off the runners-up spot, and ran them close in the cup too. Hamilton fell to a 2-1 defeat as Alex Smith scored a double to shatter the hopes of the Lanarkshire outfit.

FRIDAY 21st APRIL 1939

Two goals from Alex Venters and one from Willie Waddell gave Rangers a 3-2 win over a spirited Hamilton Accies side at Ibrox in the penultimate match of the 1938/39 league season to complete their home fixtures undefeated, with the title already in the bag by that point. Even after being defeated by Aberdeen the following week, Bill Struth could look back with satisfaction on a season in which his team had won the First Division by 11 points from closest challengers Celtic.

SATURDAY 21st APRIL 1934

Poor St Mirren were on the receiving end of a peerless display from Rangers, who dominated the Scottish game in the 1933/34 season, losing only twice in the entire campaign as they ran to a league and cup double. It was the Saints from Paisley who bore the brunt in the Scottish Cup Final – hammered 5-0 by a rampant Gers side without regular goalkeeper Dawson. Stand-in shot-stopper Hamilton wasn't tested as Nicholson, with a double, McPhail, Main and Smith thrilled a crowd of 113,403 with their goals.

SATURDAY 21st APRIL 1923

The First Division was won with a game to spare as Rangers defeated Kilmarnock 1-0 in the penultimate fixture of the league season, with Geordie Henderson scoring the all-important goal. It was another home win to add to the impressive collection, with no visitors to Govan managing to claim full points through the season.

WEDNESDAY 21st APRIL 1948

Billy "Sailor" Williamson made a heroic return to the team as he scored the only goal of the Scottish Cup Final replay against Morton in front of 133,750 at Hampden. Williamson, a former Royal Navy serviceman, had been absent from Bill Struth's side since October 1947 but was recalled for the cup replay and responded in style. The initial game had ended level at 1-1 just four days earlier, a game in which Torry Gillick was on target for Struth's team.

SATURDAY 21st APRIL 1962

Struggling St Mirren provided the opposition in the Scottish Cup Final as the Buddies battled to avoid relegation from the First Division. Goals from Ralphie Brand and Davy Wilson saw Scot Symon's side through in the end. It completed a cup double for the Gers, who had lifted the League Cup earlier in the season – but there was to be no league joy to providing the icing on the cake. In the wake of the cup final success, Rangers dropped three points in two First Division fixtures – the margin by which Dundee won the championship.

SATURDAY 21st APRIL 2001

Dens Park was the venue for one of Scottish football's oddities as Rangers played their first match in the post-split SPL. The top flight was divided into two halves of six for the last five matches for the first time in 2000/01 and the Gers beat Dundee 3-0 on the landmark date, with goals from Rod Wallace, Tore Andre Flo and Jorg Albertz. Celtic, Hibs, Kilmarnock and Hearts were the other top six contenders.

SATURDAY 22nd APRIL 1950

Scot Symon would prove a successful manager of Rangers – but it was with East Fife that he first made waves as a coach. He led the unfancied Methil outfit to the League Cup during his six years in charge but could not claim the Scottish Cup when he faced Rangers in the final in 1950. Instead the Ibrox players celebrated as Willie Thornton's double and a goal from Willie Findlay gave Bill Struth's team a 3-0 victory.

SATURDAY 23rd APRIL 1949

The second leg of the historic 1948/49 treble, the first in the club's history, was completed at Hampden Park with a 4-1 victory over relegation threatened Clyde in the Scottish Cup Final. Two George Young penalties and goals from Billy Williamson and Jimmy Duncanson did the damage. It was Williamson's second game after a five-month absence – but also his second Scottish Cup Final goal in two seasons.

SATURDAY 23rd APRIL 1960

It was a day to remember for the Rangers players who took to the field at Hampden and beat Kilmarnock 2-0 in the Scottish Cup Final – but one to forget for Harold Davis, the Iron Man of Ibrox. Davis played in every round of the competition up to that point but suffered an injury in the semi-final against Celtic and had to sit out the Killie showdown. His place was taken by veteran Ian McColl and with only 11 medals struck for the winning side there was to be no reward for Davis as Jimmy Millar's double clinched the silverware.

SUNDAY 23rd APRIL 2000

Rangers took to the field at McDiarmid Park to face St Johnstone already in party spirit. Celtic's draw against Hibs the previous day had ensured Dick Advocaat's side were crowned champions without kicking a ball against Saints, but they had the bubbly flowing with a spirited 2-0 win courtesy of a double from Billy Dodds. A 2-0 victory at Dundee United the previous weekend had laid the foundations for the celebrations. Rangers had stretched out a 21-point lead over runners-up Celtic.

SATURDAY 24th APRIL 1976

It took Derek Johnstone just 22 seconds to score against Dundee United, his boyhood heroes, when Rangers travelled to Tannadice looking for a win to clinch the inaugural Premier Division title. Johnstone's early effort proved to be the only goal of the game as the Light Blues held the Tangerines at bay to earn the two points that gave Jock Wallace's side consecutive championships.

SATURDAY 25th APRIL 1925

Airdrie were the main challengers to Rangers for the First Division honours in the 1924/25 season and it took until the final afternoon of the season for the destiny of the trophy to be settled. A 1-0 win at Ibrox against Ayr United ensured blue would be the colour of the ribbons on the silverware, with Billy McCandless getting the only goal of the game. While the leaders were doing the business in Glasgow, Airdrie slipped to a 1-0 defeat at St Johnstone to give their illustrious rivals a three-point lead at the head of the table.

SATURDAY 25th APRIL 1931

Victory was all that mattered when Rangers and their supporters travelled cross country to tackle East Fife on the final day of the 1930/31 season. Two points would guarantee the First Division trophy would rest once again in the Ibrox trophy room and the Fifers, who propped up the top-flight table, were blown away as Bob McPhail, Alex Smith, Jimmy Marshall and Sandy Archibald hit four without reply to consign Celtic to the runners-up spot as the free scoring Gers made it five-in-a-row.

WEDNESDAY 25th APRIL 1934

A trip to Brockville presented the opportunity to win the First Division for Bill Struth's side. Their 3-1 victory over Falkirk, with a double from Smith and a goal from Marshall, put Rangers out of sight of second-placed Motherwell and rounded off an impressive season in which they had not lost a single game at home. While Motherwell ended up four points off the pace, third-placed Celtic were 19 short of the target set by their city rivals.

SATURDAY 25th APRIL 1903

Hearts and Rangers were difficult to separate in 1902/03, with the men from Glasgow finishing third in the league and just a single place and single point ahead of their Edinburgh adversaries. It was a similar story in the Scottish Cup when the two sides met in the final, drawing 1-1 in the first match and then 0-0 in the replay. It took a second rematch to settle that season's competition, with Mackie and Hamilton scoring to give William Wilton's side a 2-0 victory.

SATURDAY 25th APRIL 1964

Scot Symon had his eye firmly on the treble when he took his men to Hampden for the Scottish Cup Final against Dundee. The League Cup and championship were already in the bag when Jimmy Millar, with a brace, and Ralphie Brand grabbed the goals that gave the favourites a 3-1 victory and completed the clean sweep of domestic honours. Along the way to the final, Celtic had been beaten 2-0 in the quarter-finals while minnows Duns were hammered 9-0 in the second round.

THURSDAY 26th APRIL 2007

Evidence of a conveyor belt of talent beginning to emerge from Murray Park was thrust under the spotlight as Rangers trounced Celtic 5-0 in the Scottish Youth Cup Final at Hampden. Andrew Shinnie set the ball rolling with the opener after four minutes before Steven Lennon grabbed a hat-trick and skipper Dean Furman rounded off the scoring. It was an emphatic win for the boys in blue and a result that Celtic coach John McLaughlan described as "embarrassing".

THURSDAY 26th APRIL 2012

Strathclyde Police warned they would take action against anyone found guilty of threatening members of the SFA judiciary panel which had hammered Rangers just days earlier, with sanctions including a 12-month transfer embargo imposed in response to the financial problems gripping the club during the period of administration. Outraged Gers fans later marched on Hampden to protest against the plans, but police were concerned that some would take direct action.

SATURDAY 27th APRIL 1929

Struggling Dundee proved no match for champions Rangers as the party in Govan reached full swing during a 3-0 victory. Goals from Marshall, Fleming and Bob McPhail ensured the season ended on a high to match the euphoria of the championship win – with a 16-point lead over Celtic by the time the dust settled. Bill Struth's team had gone through the 38-game programme with just a single defeat, away to Hamilton, against their name.

SATURDAY 27th APRIL 1957

The 1956/57 championship was won at Palmerston Park in Dumfries as Max Murray, with a double, and Johnny Hubbard's penalty ensured a 3-0 victory against relegation-threatened Queen of the South and ensured the Light Blues were clear of the chasing Hearts. It had been an impressive run to the finish line, with the last defeat coming on 12th January when Ayr United produced a shock at Somerset Park with a 1-0 victory over the league leaders.

WEDNESDAY 27th APRIL 1966

Popular Danish defender Kai Johansen etched his name into Ibrox folklore when he rifled home the only goal of the Scottish Cup Final replay against Celtic in front of 98,202 at Hampden. The first game, just four days earlier, ended 0-0 and the replay proved another closely contested affair. There was only one change to the team, with George McLean coming into the team at the expense of Jim Forrest, but it was the Dane who proved the hero. Johansen retired in 1970 and moved into coaching in South African football, returning to Scotland later in life to concentrate on business commitments. He died in 2007 after suffering from cancer.

WEDNESDAY 27th APRIL 2011

Newly adopted Ibrox anthem Penny Arcade rose to the top of the HMV download music chart thanks to its popularity among Rangers fans. The song, written by Sammy King and best known as a Roy Orbison hit in the 1960s, became part and parcel of matchdays and also served as a fundraising vehicle for the appeal among supporters to raise funds for the Erskine veterans' charity.

WEDNESDAY 28th APRIL 1920

No goals and only 6,000 people in the ground, but it was a day of celebration for Rangers as the Scottish championship was confirmed with a 0-0 draw away to Dumbarton. The result put William Wilton's team three points clear of Celtic with one game to play, although the title was already assured due to the superior goal difference going into the match against the Sons. It was Wilton's last honour before handing over to Bill Struth.

SUNDAY 28th APRIL 1996

Paul Gascoigne took centre stage as he produced arguably the greatest display of his Rangers career with a stunning hat-trick against Aberdeen at Ibrox in a 3-1 win. The result won the championship for Walter Smith's side with a game to spare, making it eight-in-a-row for the Light Blues. The Dons were determined to spoil the party and took the lead through Brian Irvine – but were ripped apart by Gazza, who scored with an imperious chip to equalise before embarking on a spellbinding 50-yard solo run for his second. He converted a penalty to complete his treble and start the party.

SATURDAY 29th APRIL 1933

Anything other than a heavy defeat to Hamilton on the final day of the season would give Rangers the First Division trophy. Bill Struth's men responded with a 4-2 win against the Accies at Douglas Park to finish the job, with Bob McPhail scoring twice and Fleming and Marshall on target for the hosts. Motherwell finished three points behind the champions, who hadn't lost a single home game and were beaten just twice in their 38 league fixtures.

SATURDAY 29th APRIL 1961

Relegated Ayr United were standing between Rangers and the First Division prize, with Kilmarnock, managed by Ibrox legend Willie Waddell, chasing hard on their heels going into the last game of the term. The well-oiled Gers machine showed no sign of stalling as they demolished the Honest Men 7-3 in Govan with a hat-trick from Alex Scott and doubles from Wilson and Ralph Brand – on an afternoon on which the score could easily have been doubled. The win left Rangers one point ahead of Kilmarnock at full time.

WEDNESDAY 29th APRIL 1953

Bill Struth savoured victory in the Scottish Cup for the final time during his glorious reign as Rangers manager as he steered his team to a single goal victory over Aberdeen at Hampden. It took a replay to decide the destiny of the famous piece of silverware, with the sides finishing level at 1-1 after the initial game four days earlier. Billy Simpson scored the decisive goal in the replay, having missed the first match through injury. He was restored to the side at the expense of his deputy Paton.

SATURDAY 29th APRIL 1978

The thrilling 1977/78 Premier Division race went right to the wire as Aberdeen, led by Billy McNeill, pushed Jock Wallace and Rangers all the way. The title was decided on the last day of the season as Rangers beat Motherwell 2-0 at Ibrox with goals from Colin Jackson and Gordon Smith to edge two points clear of the chasing Dons and take the trophy back from Celtic's grasp.

TUESDAY 29th APRIL 1986

Scotland had a new striker to hang their hat on as Ally McCoist stepped up to international level for the first time. His debut on this day ended in a 0-0 draw against the Netherlands in a friendly fixture in Eindhoven as Alex Ferguson handed him his first cap. McCoist's first international goals came when he notched a double against Hungary in September the following year, the first of 19 he would score in Scotland colours in 61 appearances for his country.

SATURDAY 30th APRIL 1921

When the last ball of the last game of the First Division season was kicked by Rangers at Stark's Park in Kirkcaldy it brought to an end a sweet league campaign. In 42 matches against the country's best teams they had been beaten just once, on New Year's Day by Celtic, and the 1-0 victory against hosts Raith Rovers on the closing day, thanks to Dixon's effort, was the 34th victory of the term. It gave Bill Struth's team a ten-point lead over Celtic.

SATURDAY 30th APRIL 1927

The final whistle sounded to bring the 1926/27 season to a close and it was Rangers who sat proudly at the top of the pile, five points clear of runners-up Motherwell in the league. The season had been rounded off with a 1-0 victory over Kilmarnock, thanks to Fleming's goal, and turned out to be the first of five consecutive championships that the club would win under Bill Struth's careful stewardship.

SATURDAY 30th APRIL 1949

Only a win would be good enough to win the league when Rangers travelled to face the already relegated Albion Rovers on the final day of the 1948/49 First Division season. Rovers had won just three games all season and were never likely to cause an upset, with Bill Struth's side running out 4-1 winners thanks to Willie Thornton's hat-trick and Duncanson's goal to pip runners-up Dundee to the big prize by just a single point and claiming the first treble in the history of the club.

RANGERS
On This Day

MAY

MONDAY 1st MAY 1950

Hibs had led the First Division for almost two months when they completed their fixtures – but rivals Rangers were level on points and still had a game to play. That was across the city at Cathkin Park against Third Lanark and it ended 2-2, with goals from Billy Williamson and Willie Paton, to give Bill Struth the single point he needed to edge his team ahead of the Easter Road outfit and retain the championship won the previous term.

SATURDAY 1st MAY 1976

Jock Wallace completed his first treble with Rangers as he watched his well drilled outfit beat Hearts 3-1 in the Scottish Cup Final at Hampden. Derek Johnstone's double and an Alex MacDonald goal ensured the old trophy was bound for Ibrox, with Wallace celebrating victory against the team he served as assistant manager prior to his switch to Glasgow to join Willie Waddell's coaching team. More than 85,000 were inside the national stadium to witness the trophy hat-trick being clinched.

MONDAY 1st MAY 1978

Derek Johnstone was presented with the Player of the Year prize at the Scottish Football Writers' Association annual dinner in Glasgow after an impressive season for Jock Wallace's treble-winning side. Johnstone, who scored 37 goals in domestic competition, made it a double when he was named as the Scottish Professional Footballers' Association Player of the Year to confirm his place as the toast of the nation. It was the type of form that persuaded John Greig to install the versatile star as captain.

SATURDAY 2nd MAY 1987

Graeme Souness led Rangers to the championship for the first time in his tenure as his side clinched the title with a 1-1 draw against Aberdeen at Pittodrie – and, as usual, it was done with a touch of controversy. The player-manager was sent off in a stormy encounter with the Dons but his side were already on their way to a title party by then, with captain Terry Butcher scoring the goal that ensured the Light Blues left the north-east with a point in the bag.

SATURDAY 2nd MAY 1992

A trip to face Aberdeen was what the fixture computer threw up for Rangers in the final game of 1991/92 and, if previous form had been repeated, it could have been a title decider. In the end, the prize was already winging its way to the Ibrox trophy cabinet and it was Hearts, not the Dons, who were the closest challengers. When Rangers beat Aberdeen 2-0 with an Ally McCoist double on the last day of the season, it secured a nine-point victory for Walter Smith's team.

SUNDAY 2nd MAY 1999

There could be no sweeter place to win a championship than Celtic Park. Amazingly, it was not until 1999 that Rangers savoured that sensation, giving Dick Advocaat the title in his first season in charge. In the end the margin was not close, with the would-be winners running out 3-0 winners as Neil McCann's double and a Jorg Albertz penalty sealed the all-important victory. There were three more games to play, with Rangers eventually finishing the term six points clear at the top, but the decisive one was the most celebrated of them all.

TUESDAY 3rd MAY 1938

King George VI and Queen Elizabeth visited Ibrox to formally open the Glasgow Empire exhibition that was being staged at nearby Bellahouston Park. Around 100,000 spectators watched the event at the stadium as the visitors went down a storm with the city's royalists.

WEDNESDAY 3rd MAY 1978

After months of debate, the pundits were put out of their misery when Scotland boss Ally MacLeod unveiled the 22-man squad he believed was going to conquer the globe at that summer's World Cup in Argentina. Named on his list were Rangers favourites Derek Johnstone, Tom Forsyth and Sandy Jardine as well as former Ibrox idol Willie Johnston, who was with West Brom by that point. MacLeod was adamant he had the talent at his disposal to make a major impact on the world stage, the confidence which led to the now infamous Hampden send-off for Ally's Army.

SATURDAY 4th MAY 1940

The hastily convened Scottish Emergency War Cup came to its conclusion in front of a crowd of 90,000 at Hampden Park as football was adjusted to fit with the Second World War effort. Rangers overcame Alloa Athletic, Falkirk, St Mirren and then Hibs in the semi-finals before tackling Dundee United in the final. United were defeated 1-0 as Smith did the damage for Bill Struth's team to lift morale in the blue half of Glasgow.

SATURDAY 4th MAY 2002

The sun was the shining, the fans were in full voice and the stage was set for a Scottish Cup classic. Rangers defeated Celtic 3-2 in a pulsating encounter at Hampden courtesy of a double from Peter Lovenkrands and a strike from the dominant Barry Ferguson, who covered every blade of grass on the national stadium pitch as his team twice came from behind, conceding goals to John Hartson and Bobo Balde, before Lovenkrands headed a dramatic last-minute winner to give Alex McLeish a win to savour.

SATURDAY 5th MAY 1973

Tam "Jaws" Forsyth gave the end-of-season Old Firm finale some bite with his dramatic winner in the Scottish Cup Final in front of 122,714 Old Firm fans at Hampden. Derek Parlane and Alfie Conn were also on target in the 3-2 win as Jock Wallace, in his first season as manager, tackled his last chance at ending the campaign with a trophy in the bag and ensured there was no lasting hangover from the disappointment of losing out to Celtic by a single point in the race for the championship.

SATURDAY 5th MAY 2007

The welcome mat was rolled out for a unique party of visitors at Ibrox. Rangers welcomed Scotland's religious leaders as they took in the Old Firm encounter as part of a factfinding mission. Senior figures from the Church of Scotland, Catholic church, Muslim, Hindu and Sikh faiths all attended the fixture. During their time at the ground they were briefed on the club's community initiatives, designed to bring people from the city's various religious communities together.

SATURDAY 5th MAY 1990

The 1989/90 season ended and Rangers were once again on top. A 1-1 draw at Hearts, when Stuart Munro scored a rare goal, rounded off the campaign and gave the Gers a seven-point margin over the third-placed Jambos, who finished level with runners-up Aberdeen. More significantly, it was the last time manager Graeme Souness would savour a title success as he had moved on to Liverpool by the time the following term's championship was clinched.

MONDAY 6th MAY 1963

There were still seven games First Division games remaining when Rangers made the short trip to Broomfield to tackle Airdrie. A win would be enough to clinch the title with a month to spare and Scot Symon's side duly delivered as Jim Baxter and Ralph Brand scored in a 2-0 victory. It put the prize out of reach of Kilmarnock, who ended the season nine points behind the winners. Rangers went through the league campaign undefeated at Ibrox and lost only twice on the road.

SATURDAY 6th MAY 1978

Jock Wallace signed off in style as, in the final season of his first spell in charge at Ibrox, he clinched another glorious treble with a 2-1 victory over Aberdeen in the Scottish Cup Final. Alex MacDonald and Derek Johnstone scored the goals in front of more than 61,500 people at Hampden. Wallace had overcome his old side Berwick Rangers in the third round before steering his team past Stirling Albion, Kilmarnock and Dundee United along the way to the final against the Dons.

THURSDAY 7th MAY 1953

Rangers travelled south to Dumfries knowing exactly what they needed to do to win the league. Hearts were top of the table on 43 points having completed their league programme, with Rangers, on 42, playing their game in hand against Queen of the South. With a superior goal difference, a point would be good enough for Bill Struth's men and that's exactly what they delivered as Willie Waddell scored in the 1-1 draw that took the First Division trophy back to Ibrox.

WEDNESDAY 7th MAY 1997

Nine-in-a-row turned from dream to reality with a flash of Brian Laudrup's head at Tannadice. The Great Dane's powerful header gave his team a 1-0 victory and won the historic title with a game to spare. A campaign that had started with a 1-0 win against Raith Rovers had reached the perfect conclusion at the home of the Arabs, sending Walter Smith and his team of seasoned professionals into the ranks of Ibrox immortals as they completed the quest that had become the centre of attention in the Scottish game.

THURSDAY 7th MAY 1998

What a difference a year makes. Just 12 months after the joy of nine-in-a-row, Walter Smith announced he had signed a new two-year contract with Rangers to take the reserve and youth teams. With Dick Advocaat already appointed to take over as manager in time for 1998/99, the revised duties were viewed as a way of tapping into Smith's experience and knowledge without interfering with the new manager's overhaul of the ageing squad he had inherited.

SATURDAY 8th MAY 1943

Rangers discovered a new way to win when they came up against Falkirk in the final of the Southern League Cup. Bill Struth's team couldn't be separated from the Bairns during 90 minutes in the war-time competition at Hampden, with Torry Gillick scoring during a 1-1 draw, so the match went down to corners – Rangers taking the prize by virtue of an 11-3 advantage when the flag kicks were tallied up.

SATURDAY 9th MAY 1942

Rangers continued to keep spirits high as the war dominated life for everyone in Britain. Having defeated Celtic 2-0 in the semi-final of the Southern League Cup, Rangers went on to lift the prize with a 1-0 victory over Morton thanks to Torry Gillick's intervention. That contribution gave the Ibrox marksman a perfect record in the competition, his eighth goal in eight matches in the cup that term – on top of the 20 he had notched in 24 Southern League appearances.

SATURDAY 9th MAY 1992

Would Ibrox hero Alex MacDonald come back to haunt his former club for Airdrie against Rangers in the Scottish Cup Final of 1992? The answer was no, but his Diamonds proved sharp enough to frustrate and repel Walter Smith's side for large chunks of the game. The old Mark Hateley and Ally McCoist double act eventually won the day, with a goal from each helping secure a 2-1 victory and the first Scottish Cup triumph since 1981.

MONDAY 9th MAY 1949

In the days before European competition, Rangers stretched their football legs by embarking on overseas tours. They kicked off a Scandinavian adventure when they defeated Swedish side Malmo in the first of a three-game trip that also included a foray into Denmark to beat Staevnet 2-0 and lose 2-1 to Akadmisk. Findlay scored in each of the games, with Willie Thornton also on target against Staevnet.

SUNDAY 9th MAY 1982

If ever there was an advertisement for the merits of a footballer dedicating themselves to their profession then surely Sandy Jardine would be the star. The talented and dependable defender celebrated his testimonial, wearing his familiar number two shirt as Southampton provided the opposition. Gordon Dalziel scored the only goal of the game to give Jardine a win on his big day, before he moved on to Hearts and embarked on the next chapter of his illustrious career. With the Jambos he smashed through the 1,000-game barrier and was crowned Scottish Football Writers' Association Player of the Year in 1986.

TUESDAY 9th MAY 2000

Rangers officials arrived in Australia to conclude a deal that would see the club take a controlling interest in Northern Spirit. Chairman David Murray viewed the move into Australian football as another step towards establishing Rangers as a global brand, envious of Manchester United's worldwide reach and marketing potential in foreign lands. With Socceroos Craig Moore and Tony Vidmar already on the Ibrox books, it was seen as a viable source of talent for the Gers as they looked to establish an overseas feeder club.

SUNDAY 9th MAY 2010

The final day of the season brought a carnival atmosphere as Rangers prepared to lift the SPL trophy. A 3-3 draw against Motherwell, with the Steelmen equalising in the dying moments, was enough to edge over the line and ensure skipper Davie Weir was able to get his hands on the trophy his team had retained in the most difficult of circumstances as they overcame financial restrictions and off-field uncertainties.

WEDNESDAY 10th MAY 2006

Dean Furman is a name that will mean little to most Rangers supporters but he does have a slice of Ibrox history to call his own. When the South African teenager signed from Chelsea on this day he became the first player recruited by new manager Paul Le Guen and arrived with a ringing endorsement from Stamford Bridge coach Steve Clarke. The midfielder, who was just 18 when he signed, failed to make an impact and was later released.

SATURDAY 11th MAY 1991

It was win or bust for Aberdeen when they travelled to face Rangers in the final game of the 1990/91 season. Locked on 53 points with their hosts at the top of the table, the stakes were high. Who would have the nerve to see it through to the end? The answer was simple: Rangers. Rookie goalkeeper Michael Watt had a torrid afternoon trying to keep the hosts at bay and was beaten twice by the impressive Mark Hateley, giving the Ibrox men a 2-0 victory and a two-point winning margin in the race of the title.

SATURDAY 12th MAY 1945

With the war still truncating football in Scotland, Rangers kept their hand in with victory in the Southern League Cup's Section A as they faced up to Motherwell in the final at Hampden. Torry Gillick and Alex Venters were on target in the 2-1 victory over the Steelmen in a match that attracted almost 70,000 people to the national stadium. The Gers had already beaten Celtic to the Southern League title the previous month, with Well also challenging for the championship before having to settle for third spot.

RANGERS CELEBRATE WINNING ANOTHER TITLE IN MAY 2010

TUESDAY 12th MAY 1981

Rangers hammered Dundee United 4-1 in the Scottish Cup Final replay at Hampden, just three days after the teams had failed to score a goal between them in the first tie. Both games were played at the national stadium, with the replay crowd of 43,099 more than 10,000 down on the initial attendance. On target for John Greig's side on the day were John McDonald, with a double, Davie Cooper and Bobby Russell. It was Rangers' second replay of the Scottish Cup campaign that term, with St Johnstone overcome after two ties in the fourth-round.

SATURDAY 13th MAY 1995

The curtain fell on 1994/95 with a 1-1 draw at home to Partick Thistle, with Craig Moore on target. By then the title was already in the bag, but the result gave Rangers a 15-point margin over runners-up Motherwell. Well, who beat the Gers twice in the league that term, had been the closest challengers throughout the business end of the season, with Celtic trailing home fourth and Hibs finishing third. The run towards nine-in-a-row continued, seven down and two to go.

SATURDAY 14th MAY 1994

Just two points from the last five games of the 1993/94 season does not sound like championship-winning form, but Rangers had done enough earlier in the campaign to clinch the league ahead of challengers Aberdeen. The campaign drew to a close on 14th May with a 0-0 draw at home to Dundee and that draw ensured the Ibrox men ended the term three points clear of the Dons as they made it six-in-a-row.

WEDNESDAY 14th MAY 2008

Fully 36 years after the glory of Barcelona, a new generation of Rangers stars set out to propel themselves into the realms of legends by leading the club to European success. The Uefa Cup Final in Manchester paired them with former Ibrox boss Dick Advocaat and his Zenit St Petersurg side and it was the Russians who came out on top, winning 2-0 to shatter the dreams of Walter Smith's side after their brave and spirited run to the final.

WEDNESDAY 15th MAY 1963

Rangers were bidding to retain the Scottish Cup when they went toe to toe with their Old Firm rivals in the final. The initial game, on 4th May, ended locked at 1-1 but the replay was a one-sided affair as Celtic were swept aside with a Ralphie Brand double and Jimmy Wilson goal as Scot Symon's side breezed to a 3-0 win and lifted the silverware in some style in front of a crowd of 120,273.

SATURDAY 15th MAY 1993

A 2-1 win at Falkirk wrapped up the 1992/93 league season, the final match of a marathon 44-game campaign. Alexei Mikhailichenko and Mark Hateley scored the goals that afternoon and had been key players that term – particularly Hateley, with his 21-goal haul in the league. Still it was not enough to topple Ally McCoist from the top of the scoring chart after his 34-goal contribution. The league was won with a nine-point advantage over Aberdeen.

SUNDAY 15th MAY 2011

Walter Smith made it a perfect ten, as he bowed out of the Rangers manager's chair with his tenth and final league championship victory. It was done in some style, with an impressive 5-1 victory at Kilmarnock on an afternoon on which victory was imperative to guarantee the prize. Any thoughts of another dramatic Helicopter Sunday were blasted away as the imperious Rangers side swept Killie aside and coasted over the finish line with a hat-trick for Kyle Lafferty and goals from Steven Naismith and Nikica Jelavic capping a memorable swansong for the godfather of Ibrox.

SUNDAY 16th MAY 1954

Rangers ran out in the Canadian city of Montreal to face English opponents Chelsea at the start of a three-week North American sojourn. The team played matches in Toronto and Ontario while in Canada and also moved across the US border to tackle Chelsea again in New York. They played local opposition during their stay but also faced Chelsea in three exhibition matches, winning one and losing another as well as drawing 0-0 in the final encounter.

FRIDAY 16th MAY 1986

Colin West was not the most expensive signing at Ibrox nor the most successful, but he was very significant. West became the first man recruited by Graeme Souness as the revolution began at Ibrox. The 23-year-old striker cost £200,000 when he joined from Watford and was awarded a three-year contract by the rookie boss. The 6ft 2in forward had played alongside Ally McCoist previously at Sunderland.

SATURDAY 16th MAY 1998

Walter Smith's first Ibrox reign came to a disappointing end as his hopes of bowing out with a trophy were dashed by Hearts at Celtic Park. The Jambos won the Scottish Cup Final 2-1 to ensure the 1997/98 season was a barren one for Rangers. The match also marked the changing of the guard in a playing sense as Andy Goram, Ally McCoist, Ian Durrant, Richard Gough and Stuart McCall made their final appearances – McCoist signing off with a goal for at least a small consolation on a painful day.

SATURDAY 17th MAY 1941

The first ever Southern League Cup was claimed by Rangers after a replay against Hearts in front of 70,000 at Hampden. The Glasgow team beat their Edinburgh opponents 4-2 courtesy of goals from Alex Venters, Smith, Willie Thornton and Johnston having drawn the initial tie 1-1 a week earlier. The competition had been introduced to continued cup football during the war years and would be won five times in seven attempts by Rangers – who made every final during the competition's existence.

SATURDAY 17th MAY 1969

Colin Stein entered Scotland folklore as he bagged four goals against Cyprus at Hampden in a World Cup qualifier. Bobby Brown's side destroyed their visitors 8-0 and the Rangers striker was at the heart of that, scoring his first in the 29th minute and adding three more after the break as he netted in the 49th, 59th and 67th minutes. Stein, who remains the last man to score four for the national team, went on to score a total of nine goals for Scotland in 21 appearances.

SATURDAY 18th MAY 1996

Gordon "Jukebox" Durie was on song in becoming the first Ranger to score a Scottish Cup Final hat-trick. His treble came in a 5-1 demolition of Hearts at Hampden, with Brian Laudrup producing a five-star display to match and adding two goals while tormenting the Edinburgh side. Durie's contribution was the first Scottish Cup hat-trick since Dixie Deans did the same in Celtic's 6-1 win over Hibs in 1972.

TUESDAY 19th MAY

Rangers concluded the signing of Dutch defender Artur Numan from PSV Eindhoven and broke the Scottish transfer record in the process, paying £5m. Numan proved a sound investment and became new manager Dick Advocaat's first signing – but far from the last as Advocaat set about a major spending spree that would see Numan joined by a colony of his countrymen. Giovanni Van Bronckhorst was also recruited over the summer as well as Argentine forward Gabriel Amato, Daniel Prodan, Andrei Kanchelskis, Rod Wallace and Lionel Charbonnier amongst others,

SUNDAY 20th MAY 1956

Spain was the destination as the Ibrox players flew to the continent for a spot of post-season sunshine. On this day they drew 1-1 with Valencia to kick-off a five-game tour that also included a 3-0 defeat at Barcelona. Rangers faced Valencia three times in a fortnight and came away with two 1-1 draws and a 4-1 defeat against their hosts. The other match was a 2-1 win against De Mahon.

THURSDAY 21st MAY 1891

In their first Scottish Football League season, Rangers were declared joint champions of the country along with Dumbarton in one of the most unusual climaxes to any season in more than 130 years since then. The clubs had finished level on points and contested a play-off match for the championship on 21st May in front of 10,000 people at Cathkin Park – but even then they couldn't be separated, drawing 2-2. No coin tosses, no penalty shoot-out, no totting up of corners – instead the league chiefs decided the prize would be shared in the inaugural SFL season.

SUNDAY 22nd MAY 2005

Helicopter Sunday, as it will forever be known. Celtic led the SPL by two points going in to the last day of 2004/05 but could not have guessed the dramatic way the term would end. When Nacho Novo scored what proved the only goal of the game against Hibs at Easter Road in the 59th minute, Celtic were beating Motherwell by the same margin and remained on course for the title. Everything changed in the dying minutes of the season when Scott McDonald's late double for Well turned the league on its head, consigning Celtic to a 2-1 defeat and giving Rangers a 93 points to 92 SPL win on a tumultuous afternoon.

TUESDAY 23rd MAY 1978

Scottish football was rocked to its core as Jock Wallace announced his resignation from the Rangers manager's job. The coach appeared set for a lucrative move to Leicester City. Ally MacLeod, Jim McLean and Alex Ferguson were among the names tipped to take over but the following day a deal was struck with John Greig,

WEDNESDAY 24th MAY 1972

The date on which history was made: Rangers 3 Dynamo Moscow 2. That victory in the European Cup Winners' Cup Final at the Nou Camp in Barcelona has become part of Ibrox folklore and made the 11 men who ran out in the famous jersey that night legends. Willie Johnston's double and Colin Stein's goal were the obvious highlights in a match that sent pulses racing and nerves jangling. Willie Waddell's line-up for the most memorable of matches read: McCloy, Jardine, Mathieson, Greig, Johnstone, Smith, McLean, Conn, Stein, MacDonald, Johnston.

FRIDAY 24th MAY 2002

Broxi Bear followed the lead of his trophy-winning Ibrox colleagues when he lifted the Mascots Cup. The event, staged and screened by the Disney Channel, pitted English and Scottish club mascots against each other and Rangers' very own furry friend raced to the head of the field in the final. Manchester United, with Fred the Red, were the closest challengers in an epic contest.

FINAL DAY DRAMA ON HELICOPTER SUNDAY, AS MOTHERWELL BEAT CELTIC ALLOWING RANGERS THE CHANCE TO WIN THE LEAGUE WITH A 1-0 WIN OVER HIBS

SATURDAY 24th MAY 2008

Rangers bounced back from the disappointment of the Uefa Cup defeat to claim their second piece of silverware of 2007/08, clinching the Scottish Cup with a 3-2 victory against underdogs Queen of the South. A Kris Boyd double and DaMarcus Beasley's goal ensured victory.

SUNDAY 24th MAY 2009

The league was won back as Walter Smith's team dumped Dundee United 3-0 at Tannadice. Kyle Lafferty opened the scoring before Pedro Mendes and Kris Boyd completed the win to clinch the SPL prize for the first time since 2005. It was the eighth time Smith had won the league as manager, his first since returning to the club.

SUNDAY 25th MAY 2003

The 50th league crown won by Rangers was claimed in nerve shredding fashion on the final day of 2002/03 – with the SPL decided by goal difference after the Old Firm rivals ended locked on 97 points. It was Alex McLeish and his team who boasted the better record, but only by a single strike. That decisive goal came in the 6-1 victory over Dunfermline at Ibrox.

SATURDAY 26th MAY 1962

A large envelope arrived at Ibrox. Inside were 24 visas that paved the way for a groundbreaking tour behind the Iron Curtain. It gave permission for players and officials to embark on a mystery tour. The Russians were responsible for all of the arrangements, with Rangers agreeing simply to turn up. The tour comprised games against Lokomotiv Moscow, Dinamo Tblisi and Dinamo Kiev – with the games ending in 3-1 and 1-0 wins then a 1-1 draw.

SATURDAY 27th MAY 1961

The dream of landing a first continental prize ended in disappointment when Scot Symon's team fell to a 2-1 defeat against Fiorentina in the second leg of the European Cup Winners' Cup Final. Alex Scott's goal provided a crumb of comfort but the damage had been done when the Italians won 2-0 at Ibrox.

SATURDAY 27th MAY 1967

This was the day Paul Gascoigne entered the world in Gateshead. The newborn boy would go on to become one of the world's best known footballers, both for his performances on the pitch and antics off it. Gascoigne grew up in Dunston and played for Redheugh Boys' Club before being snapped up by local giants Newcastle United.

SATURDAY 27th MAY 2000

Disaster struck for Aberdeen just a minute into the Scottish Cup Final when veteran goalkeeper Jim Leighton suffered a fractured cheek. Dons manager Ebbe Skovdahl hadn't listed a replacement on the bench, so had to make do with striker Robbie Winters as a less than able deputy. Rangers took full advantage and rattled four past the helpless Pittodrie men, the goals shared between Giovanni Van Bronckhorst, Tony Vidmar, Billy Dodds and Jorg Albertz as Dick Advocaat's side completed a win that gave the club its 100th major trophy.

WEDNESDAY 28th MAY 1969

Jim Baxter came full circle as he was paraded at Ibrox on his homecoming. Sold to Sunderland for a record fee of £80,000 in 1965, Slim Jim was tempted back by new manager Davie White. He had arrived via a stop at Nottingham Forest having failed to set the heather alight in England and struggled to hit the peaks when he was put back in a Light Blue jersey by White. He was released by Willie Waddell just a year later.

MONDAY 28th MAY 1979

The disappointment of losing out to Celtic in the league in the closing weeks of 1978/79 was tempered by success in the Scottish Cup Final against Hibs, with Derek Johnstone scoring a double and Bobby Duncan netting an own goal as John Greig's side ran out 3-2 winners in the second replay. The initial final and the first replay had ended locked at 0-0, leading to three ties between the sides in the space of just 16 days. A league encounter with Hibs three days after the cup success saw the Easter Road side win 2-1 in Leith.

THURSDAY 29th MAY 1975

Jock Wallace and his players embarked on an incredible globetrotting programme when they faced up to British Columbia in a post-season tour match. The game in Vancouver ended 4-0 to the Scottish visitors, who were soon off on their travels again for a flurry of fixtures in New Zealand and Australia throughout June. The tour included two matches against the Australian national team, with the Socceroos winning 1-0 in Brisbane after being defeated 2-1 in Sydney after a Derek Parlane double.

SATURDAY 29th MAY 1999

The new look Hampden Park hosted its first Scottish Cup Final and what a day it proved. Dick Advocaat, at the end of his first season in charge, was gunning for a perfect treble and his men delivered with a hard fought 1-0 win over Celtic thanks to Rod Wallace's powerful strike from close range just five minutes into the second half to send the blue half of the city wild.

SATURDAY 29th MAY 1989

The long road to nine-in-a-row began when the first championship in that historic run was claimed in fantastic style at Ibrox. A 4-0 victory against Hearts, with doubles from English duo Mel Sterland and Kevin Drinkell, started the champagne flowing as Rangers wrested the Premier Division prize from Celtic's grasp and set off on an incredible journey that would not end until 1997. There were still three games to play in the league but the message from Graeme Souness and his assistant Walter Smith was clear: there's no room for complacency.

SATURDAY 29th MAY 1993

Walter Smith became a treble-winning Rangers manager when his charges completed the season with a 2-1 Scottish Cup triumph against Aberdeen at Celtic Park. Neil Murray and Mark Hateley did the damage as the clean sweep was concluded in front of more than 50,000 fans – including thousands of Gers fans who grabbed a slice of Parkhead history for themselves as they became the last to occupy the Jungle for a competitive game. Redevelopment work on that section of the ground began in the summer.

SUNDAY 30th MAY 1976

A five-match end of season tour of North America ended without defeat for a Rangers team fresh from their domestic treble. On this day Jock Wallace's side defeated Toronto MC 2-1 to add to the victories against American outfits Seattle Sounders and Portland Timbers. They also drew against Vancouver and Minnesota Kicks during the two-week sojourn across the Atlantic, one of a number of similar adventures during that period as links with the loyal band of fans across the pond were developed. To this day the thriving North American Rangers Supporters Association thrives, with its annual convention attracting exiled Blue Noses from across the US and Canada.

SATURDAY 30th MAY 2009

A memorable season was rounded off with a 1-0 Scottish Cup Final victory against Falkirk at Hampden. Nacho Novo scored the winning goal, adding to the Spaniard's hero status after his committed displays in the Light Blue jersey during his Ibrox career. With the league title already in the bag, Walter Smith made his a double to ensure the summer holidays could be enjoyed.

WEDNESDAY 31st MAY 1967

There were tears and frustration in Nuremberg as gallant Rangers fell 1-0 to the mighty Bayern Munich in the European Cup Winners' Cup Final. Having got the better of Irish opponents Glentoran, the Germans of Borussia Dortmund, Spanish aces Real Zaragoza and Slavia Sofia of Bulgaria there was one final hurdle to cross. It proved one match too far as Scot Symon led his team into his second continental final, having lost in the same competition in 1961 and finding a goal against the well organised Bayern side proved impossible.

MONDAY 31st MAY 1999

Vice-chairman Donald Findlay stepped down from the Ibrox board. The renowned QC, revered as one of Scotland's finest legal minds, resigned amid a row about the singing of sectarian songs at a post-match reception within Ibrox. Findlay later returned to football in 2010 when he took control at Cowdenbeath and stabilised a club which had been threatened with closure if heavy losses continued.

SATURDAY 31st MAY 2003

Alex McLeish joined an elite band of Ibrox managers when he became a treble winner to round off a fairytale first full season in charge at the club. The Scottish Cup Final against Jim Duffy's Dundee at Hampden provided the crowning glory, but a stuffy Dens side full of a cast of overseas players did their best to spoil the party. It took a headed goal mid-way through the second half from Italian stopper Lorenzo Amoruso, from a Neil McCann cross, to make it 1-0 and clinch the coveted trophy.

RANGERS
On This Day

JUNE

THURSDAY 1st JUNE 1978

Rangers star Derek Johnstone, Scotland's Player of the Year, suffered a World Cup blow when he limped out of a training session with Ally Macleod's squad in Argentina as preparations for the big kick-off entered their final phase. The Ibrox skipper had gone over on his ankle and was rated a major doubt for the tournament opener against Peru. Johnstone did not feature in the game two days later and could only watch in horror as the national side slumped to a 3-1 defeat, with Rangers team-mate Tom Forsyth in the thick of the action.

SATURDAY 2nd JUNE 1962

Rangers went behind the Iron Curtain when they accepted a unique invitation from the authorities in the USSR to travel to face local opposition. The first match, on 2nd June, was a 3-1 win against Lokomotiv Moscow in which Ian McMillan, Ralph Brand and Davy Wilson scored. Next was a trip to Georgia to face Dinamo Tblisi, a match won 1-0 thanks to Willie Henderson's goal, while a tussle with Dinamo Kiev in Ukraine, in front of 60,000 people, rounded off the intriguing overseas mission. That match ended 1-1, with Brand again on target.

TUESDAY 3rd JUNE 1986

Newly appointed player-manager Graeme Souness was pinpointed by Scotland boss Alex Ferguson as the key man at the World Cup finals in Mexico. Ferguson, speaking in the build-up to the opening fixture against Denmark, had confirmed Souness as his captain and, on this day, called on the new Ibrox gaffer to use his leadership skills to stamp his authority on the tournament.

WEDNESDAY 4th JUNE 1969

There was trouble and strife for Rangers during their North American tour. Just days after Colin Stein had been sent off playing in a 4-3 defeat against Tottenham in Toronto, Willie Johnston was given his marching orders in the 4th June match against Italian aces Fiorentina at Randalls Island Stadium in New York. Rangers had the last laugh as goals from Dave Smith, Andy Penman and Stein gave them a 3-2 win with an impressive attacking display.

MONDAY 5th JUNE 1989

David Murray, already the owner of the club, became chairman. Having allowed David Holmes to continue in the role during the transition period following his takeover, the new majority shareholder decided it was time to take complete control of the day to day running of the business as he got to grips with the task facing him at Ibrox. Holmes later returned to football as managing director at Dundee.

MONDAY 6th JUNE 1983

It was on this day that Ally McCoist officially became a Rangers player as his registration was lodged with the SFA. It marked the end of a long pursuit by John Greig, who had spotted the potential in the young Sunderland striker. McCoist had joined the Roker Park club from St Johnstone in a big money deal in 1981 at a time when Greig was keen on taking him to Glasgow. A return of eight goals in 56 appearances tempted the Black Cats to allow him to return home for £185,000 two years later. The rest is Rangers history.

THURSDAY 7th JUNE 1984

Rangers rounded off their World Series campaign in Australia with a 4-2 victory over Australia B in Newcastle thanks to goals from Craig Paterson, Hugh Burns, Ally McCoist and Davie Cooper. The fixtures had been arranged as a promotional event by the host country's national federation, with Scottish coach Eddie Thompson in charge of the B team. Manchester United, Nottingham Forest, Juventus and Greek outfit Iraklis were the other teams involved.

WEDNESDAY 8th JUNE 1977

Rangers signed a six-figure cheque for the first time since Colin Stein's transfer from Hibs in 1968 as Clydebank starlet Davie Cooper was snapped up for £100,000. The 21-year-old Scotland Under-21 winger, who had won promotion to the full international squad, had turned down overtures from several English sides in favour of carving out a career in his homeland and got his reward with a dream move to Ibrox. Cooper had helped the Bankies rise from the Second Division to the Premier Division before sealing his big move.

FRIDAY 9th JUNE 1989

Admiral were unveiled as the new kit suppliers, due to take over from Umbro when that contract expired the following year. The club said the agreement was worth £4m over a four-year term, although the relationship only lasted until 1992 when Adidas took over. The news of the cash injection came just a day after a seven-figure deal to sign Trevor Steven from Everton was engineered, highlighting the need for fresh sources of funding.

FRIDAY 10th JUNE 1994

Plain old Alistair McCoist became Alistair McCoist MBE. The Queen's birthday honours list was announced and the Ibrox stalwart was among an elite band of sportsmen and women who were named. Manchester United legend Bobby Charlton was knighted while cricket star Viv Richards became an OBE and boxing's Barry McGuigan, like McCoist, was made an MBE. Other Scots on the 1994 birthday list included actor Richard Wilson and fiddler Ally Bain, awarded an MBE and OBE respectively.

MONDAY 10th JUNE 1996

Football was coming home, and Scotland were part of it. Euro 96 in England kicked off for the national team with a game against the Netherlands at Villa Park in Birmingham and the backbone of Craig Brown's team had a distinctly blue tinge to it. With Andy Goram in goal, Stuart McCall in the engine room and Gordon Durie leading the line the team produced a dogged and professional display against the Dutch to earn a 0-0 draw.

SUNDAY 11th JUNE 1978

Tom Forsyth flew the flag for Rangers as Scotland's World Cup hopes hung by a threat in Argentina. The defender was the only Ibrox player in Ally MacLeod's starting 11 for the do or die match against Holland and played admirably as the national team came up with another method of exiting the game's premier competition before the knock-out stages. Despite the spirited 3-2 win, capped by *that* goal from Archie Gemmill, the damage had been done in the earlier group games and Scotland were dumped out on goal difference, sent homewards to think again.

RANGERS KEEPER ANDY GORAM CELEBRATES A CLEAN SHEET FOR SCOTLAND AGAINST HOLLAND AT EURO 96

TUESDAY 12th JUNE 2011

Dundee United star David Goodwillie was revealed as the man at the top of new manager Ally McCoist's summer shopping list. The Arabs player was a man in demand and, after a stinging rebuke from the Tannadice board for opening the bidding too low, Rangers lost out in the auction to Blackburn Rovers after a long and drawn out attempt to secure the services of the United youth product. The failure to land the prime target raised concerns about the club's ability to compete in the transfer market, concerns that would prove justified as the troubled 2011/12 season progressed.

FRIDAY 13th JUNE 1980

Rangers were tempted across the Atlantic by the lure of a $100,000 first prize in the Red Leaf Cup and played their opening game in the tournament on this day. John Greig's side drew 3-3 with French side Nancy to get off on the right foot in a competition designed to promote plans for a new Canadian soccer league. Two days later the trip turned sour when, during a 1-0 win over a brutal Ascoli outfit from Italy, police had to wade into the crowd after violence broke out in the stands at Varsity Stadium in Toronto. There were calmer scenes on 18th June when the Gers drew 1-1 with Botafogo, of Brazil, to book a place in the final. Ascoli went on to win that match 1-0.

MONDAY 14th JUNE 1982

A reshuffle of the Ibrox coaching staff saw Tommy McLean beginning his new role as assistant to manager John Greig on this day. McLean had been cutting his teeth by coaching the youth sides at Rangers but was handed the opportunity to exert his influence on the top team. With his elder brothers Jim and Willie already established as managers in their own right, it was a logical career progression for the committed Ibrox man. As part of the reorganisation, Davie Provan, who had been heavily involved in youth coaching, was detailed to concentrate on his role as chief scout as Joe Mason took charge of the reserves alongside Stan Anderson. A replacement for physiotherapist Tommy Craig was also due to be recruited.

TUESDAY 15th JUNE 2010

David Murray announced that the club was no longer for sale, after protracted talks with potential buyer Andrew Ellis proved fruitless. Murray told supporters that recent success on the pitch, plus positive talks with bankers, had built a strong platform to move forward with a business plan which he said would provide stability under his ownership. It appeared to bring to a close the lingering doubts about the future of Rangers once and for all – but it did not take long for the takeover talk to resurface.

WEDNESDAY 16th JUNE 2004

Rangers TV was launched by chief executive Martin Bain, who unveiled a partnership with Irish broadcaster Setanta that would see the club's own programmes broadcast each weekday night to follow the lead of giants including Manchester United and Real Madrid. Celtic also launched their own channel at the same time as Setanta clinched deals with both halves of the Old Firm, although live game coverage was not part of the plan.

FRIDAY 16th JUNE 2006

Skipper Barry Ferguson became an MBE in the Queen's birthday honours list, following in the bootsteps of John Greig, Ally McCoist and Walter Smith. Ferguson, who was also captain of Scotland at the time, was recognised for his service to club and country as well as his commitment to charity causes through his involvement in the sport. He missed his date at Buckingham Palace in the autumn of that year, when he should have accepted the honour, because he was on duty with the national team in the Euro 2008 qualifiers. He was presented with his MBE at a later date.

TUESDAY 17th JUNE 2003

Portugal striker Nuno Capucho, part of Porto's Uefa Cup-winning side in 2003, agreed a two-year contract with Rangers. The 31-year-old represented a £700,000 investment by Alex McLeish – but with 34 caps under his belt looked to be a risk-free signing. Capucho was touted as a replacement for Claudio Canniggia but failed to hit the same heights as the Argentine striker had done during his time at Ibrox.

WEDNESDAY 18th JUNE 2008

John Greig accepted an honorary doctorate from Glasgow University. He and Celtic counterpart Billy McNeill were recognised for their careers in football in the city. The university said the doctorates were in honour of Greig and McNeill's outstanding football achievements and their roles as ambassadors for the sport.

SATURDAY 18th JUNE 2011

Former SFA chief executive Gordon Smith was appointed director of football at Rangers, with a brief to support and assist Ally McCoist in his team building plans. Smith was recruited by Craig Whyte along with Ali Russell, who was named director of operations and commercial activity by Whyte. Russell had served as commercial director at QPR and both men were tasked with using their experience and knowledge to help ensure the owner's first season was a memorable one. Memorable it was, but for the wrong reasons.

TUESDAY 19th JUNE 1973

A power struggle in the corridors of power at Ibrox ended when chairman John Lawrence announced his decision to step down from the top job. The statement came following a special board meeting at the ground, with Matt Taylor confirmed as Lawrence's successor. Rae Simpson was installed vice-chairman with Willie Waddell, John Wilson and Lawrence Marlborough, the grandson of the departing chairman, appointed to join the new-look board of directors. Lawrence's departure after ten years in the post came after his failure to have director David Hope named as the new chairman.

TUESDAY 20th JUNE 2006

The Paul Le Guen era officially began as the Frenchman took to the Murray Park training field for the first time, having been appointed at the end of the previous season. The former Lyon coach had touched down in Glasgow the previous day and was fresh from a one year sabbatical from the game and eager to get started on his Scottish project. With an impressive cv from his time in the French top flight he looked certain to make a big impact at Ibrox – but the impression he made was different from the one that had been anticipated.

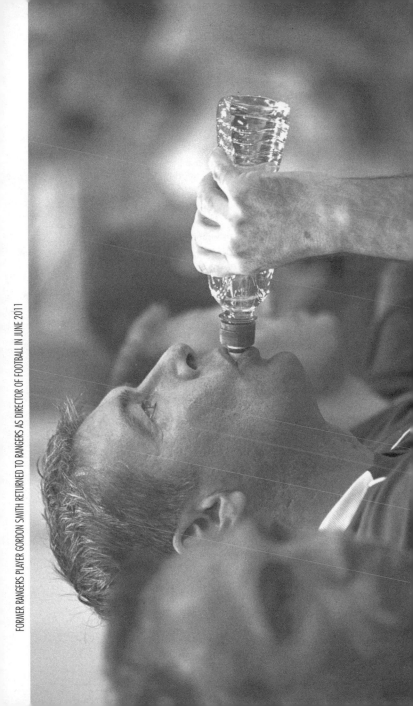

WEDNESDAY 21st JUNE 2000

Rangers agreed a fee with Hibs for promising young striker Kenny Miller, with an initial outlay of £1.5m reported, a possible £500,000 to be added depending on his success at Ibrox. Miller was just 20 at the time but jumped at the chance to switch to Glasgow and begin what proved to be a long association with the club, going on to spend two stints in Gers colours after leaving for Wolves in 2001 and then returning, via Celtic and Derby, in 2008. Miller departed for Turkish side Bursaspor in 2011

SUNDAY 22nd JUNE 1975

Jock Wallace and his team wrapped up their gruelling tour of New Zealand and Australia with a 2-1 defeat against Western Australia in Perth. The trip had included seven games spread over less than three weeks, with the highlight being a double header against the Australian national side. The first match ended in a 2-1 victory in Sydney, with Derek Parlane scoring both goals, while the hosts got their revenge with a 1-0 victory in the rematch in Brisbane.

TUESDAY 23rd JUNE 1998

Colin Hendry captained Scotland in the closing game of the country's World Cup campaign, a painful 3-0 defeat against Morocco. The national skipper played that match in St Etienne as a Blackburn Rovers employee, but within weeks his anticipated move to Rangers had come to fruition and he became one of the first bricks laid in Dick Advocaat's squad-building exercise at Ibrox. Also in the Scotland team was future Gers colleague Gordon Durie.

FRIDAY 24th JUNE 2011

Young Blues Kyle Hutton and Gregg Wylde risked incurring the wrath of the SFA when they expressed a desire to be part of Team GB for the 2012 Olympics. With Hampden chiefs adamant they wanted Scotland to play no part in providing players for the London games, the two Rangers starlets broke ranks to express their desire to push for a place in Stuart Pearce's squad for the gala occasion as the debate about the merits of a British select team raged on.

THURSDAY 25th JUNE 1987

Everton manager Colin Harvey issued a "hands off" warning to Rangers as Graeme Souness circled around Goodison midfielder Trevor Steven. Harvey said he doubted whether Rangers had enough money to purchase his star man – but was proved wrong just weeks later when Steven was confirmed as an Ibrox player in a £1m deal that saw him become a key man for the club in two stints, with a spell at Marseille sandwiched in between.

MONDAY 26th JUNE 1978

The bulldozers moved in as the first stage of an ambitious £9m redevelopment of Ibrox began. The first phase was to demolish the East terracing, which held 15,000 diehard Rangers fans, and replace it with the all-seated 7,500 capacity Copland Road stand. The plan was to repeat the exercise at the opposite end of the pitch the following year before beginning work on the rest of the ground, building towards a 47,000 capacity stadium with all but 5,000 of those fans seated.

THURSDAY 27th JUNE 1991

The man best known at The Goalie checked in at Ibrox. Signed from Hibs in a £1m deal the Scotland stopper Andy Goram had been an idol to the Easter Road fans thanks to his flamboyant heroics, but took time to win over the discerning Gers loyal. He did, though, and did it in style. After replacing Chris Woods and settling into his role, Goram's incredible displays at the heart of the Rangers rearguard established him as a legend and heart-on-sleeve favourite. He left in 1998.

WEDNESDAY 28th JUNE 1967

Rangers Enterprises was registered as a limited company. A subsidiary of Rangers Football Club, the new company was formed to extend the club's commercial reach and immediately set about investing in the three-storey premises that would house the Rangers Social Club and Rangers Pools offices. The pools had been launched in 1964 and went on to become a huge source of revenue in the decades which followed. The premises were badly damaged by fire in 1971 but rebuilt within months using insurance money.

FRIDAY 29th JUNE 2007

One of the most complicated transfer deals ever negotiated by Rangers came to an unsatisfactory conclusion as Andy Webster signed a six-month extension to his loan deal at Ibrox. Manager Walter Smith had wanted to take the Wigan defender on a permanent contract after he had impressed during an initial spell in Light Blue, but an ongoing dispute between the Scotland star and his former club Hearts made it impossible. Webster had been ordered to pay Hearts £625,000 after cancelling his Tynecastle contract to switch to Wigan but then returning to Scotland after just five games for the English side.

MONDAY 30th JUNE 1986

Chris Woods agreed the finishing touches to a contract that would make him the highest paid player in Rangers' history. The England goalkeeper, who was paraded in front of the Scottish media at Ibrox the following day, was reported to have been offered a £140,000 per year deal to switch from Norwich City to Scottish football. Only player-manager Graeme Souness was said to be on a higher salary than his new shot-stopping star. The £600,000 transfer fee represented a world record for a goalkeeper and chief executive David Holmes insisted it did not represent the end of the summer signing spree.

RANGERS
On This Day

JULY

WEDNESDAY 1st JULY 1987

Scottish Brewers officially became the new main sponsors of Rangers as the club's agreement with Fife-based glazing and conservatory company CR Smith ended. The drinks firm opted to promote their McEwan's Lager brand on the front of the Rangers strip, where it remained until being replaced by the NTL logo in 1999. The first kit to bear the McEwan's mark was the chequerboard Umbro top that became synonymous with the Graeme Souness era, while the Admiral, Adidas and first Nike design also carried the lager's name as the brewer was rewarded for its investment with massive exposure through the club's incredible run of success during that period.

SATURDAY 1st JULY 1989

Blue Noses were promised the Ibrox matchday experience would never be the same again as David Murray announced the appointment of a leading hotel executive as the chief of catering at the club. Peter Kingston, with experience from the luxury Turnberry and Gleneagles resorts, was installed and immediately promised a revamped menu featuring char-grilled burgers, pakora and jumbo hot dogs. More than £150,000 had been spent on refurbishing the snack bars in club colours, complete with red, white and blue packaging, as the club was dragged into the modern era.

TUESDAY 2nd JULY 1991

Spending £1m on a left-back sounded a big expense, but Walter Smith's investment was a shrewd one. David Robertson signed from Aberdeen to launch what proved to be one of the most glittering Rangers careers ever seen. Robertson, recruited from his hometown team Aberdeen, where he had been recruited by Alex Ferguson as a teenager, went on to win six league championship medals, the Scottish Cup three times and the League Cup. He moved to Leeds United in 1997 but retired through injury three years later, his hopes of making an impact in England hampered by the knee problem that brought his playing days to a premature end. He made a brief playing comeback with Montrose after joining the Angus side's coaching staff in 2002, going on to manage in the Third Division with Elgin City and then Montrose before moving to America to continue his coaching career.

FRIDAY 3rd JULY 1989

It was not reported at the time, but this was a significant day in the history of the Rangers Football Club. While it would be another week until the Mo Johnston signing was announced, it was on 3rd July that Graeme Souness sat his assistant Walter Smith down and canvassed his opinion on the prospects of recruiting the former Celtic star. Smith was enthusiastic and, with his trusted ally's blessing, Souness set the wheels in motion to make the deal of the century a reality.

WEDNESDAY 4th JULY 2001

Murray Park was officially opened as Rangers embraced a bold new era at the impressive training complex. Covering 38 acres at Auchenhowie, the centre features six full-size and two half-size outdoor pitches as well as an indoor facility and training base as the emphasis on producing homegrown players shifted back to manager Dick Advocaat. It was named after chairman David Murray after the board and supporters' groups made the decision.

FRIDAY 5th JULY 2002

David Murray made the shock announcement that he was standing down from the chairman's role. Vice-chairman John McClelland was named as his successor in the top job, although Murray would retain his majority stake in the club. He was to adopt the title of honorary chairman, but let McClelland, who had been acting as deputy for almost two years, take charge of the day to day running of the club and its board. The exiting chairman said it would allow him more time to devote to his main company, Murray International Holdings.

MONDAY 6th JULY 1987

Rock Steady Security unveiled plans to "revolutionise" crowd control at Rangers matches after signing a contract to provide stewards for all Ibrox games. The Edinburgh-based firm had experience of policing music crowds and also provided personal protection services to stars including Simon Le Bon but were keen to branch out into top-flight football. The company, which had managed the stewarding for Rod Stewart and Simple Minds gigs at Ibrox, was tasked with providing 200 supervisors, stewards and turnstile operators for Rangers.

MONDAY 6th JULY 1970

A new-look backroom team took to the training field for the first time as Willie Waddell's reshaped coaching staff reported for duty at Ibrox. Heading the cast was Jock Wallace, tempted to Glasgow after serving as assistant manager at Hearts. Wallace, the new head coach, was assisted by Stan Anderson and had Tom Craig as support. Craig had been brought to the club from Clyde, to serve as physiotherapist and masseur.

THURSDAY 6th JULY 2006

Paul Le Guen took charge of Rangers for the first time and got off to a winning start as his team defeated Linfield 2-0 in a Belfast friendly. Thomas Buffel opened the scoring before the match was wrapped up by Kris Boyd to get the new boss up and running. The pre-season preparations did not all run smoothly, with a tour of South Africa throwing up some disappointing results and pointing towards the amount of work still to be done by the new coach.

FRIDAY 7th JULY 1989

Graeme Souness flew to Paris with chief executive Alan Montgomery to meet with Mo Johnston and his agent Bill McMurdo. The top secret mission, conducted in a coffee shop near to Orly Airport, resulted in an agreement being struck to take the Scotland star from Nantes to Ibrox. He had been given time to consider the impact his controversial switch would have on his personal life but accepted the challenge and pledged to join Souness and his team.

TUESDAY 8th JULY 1975

The luck of the Irish shone on Rangers, who took their place in the draw for the European Cup for the first time in a decade. The Zurich event saw Jock Wallace's side plucked from the hat alongside Bohemians, of Dublin, as the first round was determined. The pairing gave the Ibrox men a good chance of progression and that proved the case when the two legs were played in September and October that year, with the Scots winning 5-2 on aggregate before crashing out at the hands of French outfit St Etienne in the second round.

KRIS BOYD WAS ON TARGET IN PAUL LE GUEN'S FIRST FRIENDLY MATCH AGAINST LINFIELD IN JULY 2006

MONDAY 9th JULY 2001

Rangers gained a new celebrity fan in flying Dutch winger Marc Overmars. The Barcelona star was spotted in the stand as the Scots tackled amateur side WHC Wezep during the pre-season training camp in the Netherlands, but was not lining up a move to Ibrox. Instead he admitted he was there simply to cheer on the Light Blues, having developed an appreciation for the finer things in Scottish football through friend and international colleague Ronald de Boer. Overmars was treated to eight goals by Dick Advocaat's side, including a hat-trick from Kenny Miller in his 45-minute appearance.

MONDAY 10th JULY 1989

The Sun broke the news that sent Scotland into a spin – Mo Johnston had shunned Celtic's advances and was destined for Ibrox. Rangers had hoped to keep the news secret until a 10am press conference at the ground, but were beaten to the punch by the red top. They went ahead with the media call and paraded their new recruit in a blaze of flash bulbs and amid a forest of microphones. History was made in the Blue Room as the most high profile Catholic ever to sign for Rangers made his entrance.

TUESDAY 10th JULY 1990

Old Blue Eyes entertained the Blue Noses when Frank Sinatra arrived at Ibrox for a concert organised by Glasgow District Council. It came during a period in which the club was keen to make more use of the ground over the summer months and attracted around 11,000 music fans. The Rat Pack favourite had been reputedly paid £600,000 for the one-off appearance, leaving the council in the red after they had budgeted for attracting 30,000.

WEDNESDAY 11th JULY 2007

Walter Smith's summer recruitment drive continued with the £2.25m acquisition of Scotland star Lee McCulloch from Wigan Athletic. Signed on a four-year contract, the 29-year-old said he was delighted to finally be joining the club he had watched as a boy. The versatile and experienced player remained on the staff after Smith's departure in 2011, proving a reliable servant to the Ibrox cause.

MONDAY 12th JULY 1982

It was the end of an era for Rangers and the start of one for Hearts as Ibrox stalwart Sandy Jardine joined the Jambos as assistant manager to his former Gers team-mate Alex MacDonald. Jardine combined his role with a place on the Tynecastle playing staff and enjoyed an Indian summer with his boyhood heroes, becoming a standout performer during his and MacDonald's successful tenure and winning the Scottish Football Writers' Association Player of the Year award in 1986 to match the one he had won with Rangers in 1975.

FRIDAY 13th JULY 2007

Friday the 13th proved anything but unlucky for Alan Hutton with the defender signing a bumper five-year contract. The deal was as important to the club as it was to the young Scotland international, ensuring he would command a healthy fee if interest from England's top flight became serious. Within six months he was on his way to Tottenham for £8m, becoming the most expensive player sold by Rangers. Hutton was later reunited with his former Ibrox gaffer Alex McLeish when he joined Aston Villa in 2011.

SATURDAY 14th JULY 1951

Remember the St Mungo Cup? It's very unlikely any Rangers supporter would. The club's involvement in the one-off competition was a 2-1 defeat at Aberdeen, putting the Ibrox men out of the summer tournament. The trophy had been instigated as Scottish football's contribution to the Festival of Britain, a nationwide celebration designed to mark the United Kingdom's contribution to arts, science, technology and industrial design.

TUESDAY 15th JULY 2008

The Rangers Ladies team was launched, ready to take its place in the Scottish Women's First Division. Formed as the result of a partnership with Paisley City Ladies, the side had former Ibrox youth coach Drew Todd at the helm and Jayne Somerville as its captain. Within three years Alana Marshall became the first player to be called up by the Scotland women's team when she was named in the squad to tackle France.

SATURDAY 15th JULY 2007

Fifteen-year-old John Fleck made his Rangers debut in a pre-season match against SV Lippstadt, matching the age at which youngsters including Derek Ferguson had been given their first taste of first team action. He made his competitive debut against East Stirling the following year and on 24th May 2008 he became the youngest player to feature in a senior British cup final when he came on in the closing stages of the 3-2 win against Queen of the South.

WEDNESDAY 15th JULY 1981

The press were given a sneak preview of the new Ibrox as the finishing touches were put to the latest stage of its redevelopment. Work completed over the summer included the installation of an undersoil heating system based on the one employed by Liverpool. The system cost £80,000 and featured a 24-mile network of hot water pipes laid nine inches below the surface of the pitch.

SUNDAY 16th JULY 2000

It was men against boys in every respect as Rangers continued their pre-season tour of the Netherlands with a friendly against Dutch amateurs Alphense Boys. In one of the most one-sided pre-season games ever encountered, the hosts conceded 12 as Allan Johnston, installed as a lone striker, bagged five on his own – including a 15-minute hat-trick. Barry Ferguson chipped in with a hat-trick, Andrei Kanchelskis scored two and Neil McCann and Kenny Miller completed the tally.

MONDAY 17th JULY 1978

Relaxed and refreshed after a summer break in Majorca, John Greig reported for work at The Albion to take charge of his first training session as Rangers manager. Derek Parlane, who had previously requested a transfer, had settled his differences with the club following Greig's appointment was the first to report for duty – but fellow striker Derek Johnstone was nowhere to be seen. Johnstone was stranded in Ibiza after flights were hit by strike action on the continent and missed the start of pre-season training. Greig had opted against the traditional gruelling return to action on the Gullane sands and instead plumped for a workout at the training ground.

FRIDAY 17th JULY 2009

The curtain finally fell on Barry Ferguson's Rangers career when he completed his £1.2m move to Birmingham City, where he was reunited with his former Ibrox and Scotland boss Alex McLeish. Ferguson, who had been stripped of the captaincy months earlier after his well publicised breach of discipline while on Scotland duty, brought to an end his second spell with the club. After joining as a schoolboy in 1994 he had moved to Blackburn in 2003 for £7.5m but returned 18 months later for £4.5m to start his second stint in Light Blue.

WEDNESDAY 18th JULY 1990

Top Man jumped into bed with Rangers as the national clothes chain's representatives arrived at Ibrox to finalise a deal that would see its 19 Scottish stores stock club merchandise which would include strips, scarves, tartan and souvenirs. It followed a pilot scheme at the Top Man stores in Ayr and Kilmarnock.

SATURDAY 19th JULY 2003

One tournament, one day, two games. That was the format for the Wernesgruner Cup as Rangers picked up some silverware on the 2003 pre-season tour of Germany. The round robin competition saw the visiting Scots tackle VFB Auerbach in the first of two 45 minute matches, hammering them 5-1 in a game featuring a Michael Mols hat-trick. The day and the competition was rounded off with a 1-0 victory against Erzgebirge in the second match of the day, with just a single Ronald de Boer goal settling things. Trialists David May and Emerson Thome had a chance to impress.

TUESDAY 20th JULY 2004

A new hero was born as new recruit Nacho Novo demonstrated he knew the way to goal as he settled into his new surroundings in the Rangers team. Novo, signed from Dundee during the summer, starred in an impressive 4-1 win over Italian giants Roma, scoring twice as the Serie A side were swept aside during the pre-season stay in Austria. Fellow new faces Dado Prso and Alex Rae were also on target as the new look Gers began to take shape.

SATURDAY 21st JULY 2001

A true Ibrox legend was honoured as Belgian outfit Anderlecht arrived in Glasgow to provide the opposition for John Brown's testimonial, trying their best to spoil the party with a 2-1 win. More than 25,000 turned out to pay homage to Bomber, a loyal servant who repaid his modest transfer fee several times over. Recruited by Graeme Souness in 1988 for £350,000 from Dundee as a 25-year-old, the versatile Dens man was a boyhood Gers fan who would have walked to Govan from Tayside to sign. Brown was signed as a midfielder but his defensive displays made him a standout performer in the nine-in-a-row team, playing through to 1996 when injury forced his retirement. He went on to serve as a youth and reserve coach until his departure during a backroom reshuffle in 2006. Brown's testimonial was to be the last under David Murray's chairmanship, with the owner stating he felt the age of the benefit game had passed.

MONDAY 22nd JULY 1968

Rangers went to the dogs, quite literally. With the traditional training ground at The Albion under redevelopment, manager Davie White came up with a novel solution to the problem of finding training facilities. He secured the use of the nearby White City greyhound stadium to put his players through their paces, wary of continuing to use the pitch at Ibrox as he had been forced to do at the start of preparations for 1968/69. The switch to White City coincided with White's introduction of double training sessions, morning and afternoon, to replace the traditional single workout.

SATURDAY 22nd JULY 1989

Mo Johnston made his keenly-awaited Rangers debut – behind closed doors, away from the curious crowds and intense scrutiny. The match in question was against Airdrie at Broomfield and the new boy proved his match fitness with a hat-trick as he pulled on Rangers colours for the first time. He made his first public appearance for the club one week later when the team returned to Airdrie to play a testimonial, and although there were no goals this time, there was no sign of a negative reaction as Johnston was applauded onto the park.

SATURDAY 23rd JULY 2011

Ally McCoist realised his dream as he led Rangers as manager for the first time. Hearts were the visitors to Ibrox on the opening day of the 2011/12 season – and the Jambos had failed to read the fairytale script. Instead of revelling in a debut victory, Super Ally was forced to read the riot act to his troops after they fell behind early on. Steven Naismith cancelled out David Obua's goal after the break to give McCoist a 1-1 draw in his first game as boss.

MONDAY 24th JULY 1989

It was announced that a touch of tartan was the latest innovation to boost the club's commercial revenue. Rangers had registered its own plaid design and commissioned Glasgow kiltmakers John Macgregor to manufacture a range using the blue, black and red fabric. Another firm, Tartan Sportswear, had been created to market the merchandise as the club looked for another niche in the football market.

WEDNESDAY 24th JULY 1996

Rangers fans were met with the news that former manager Jock Wallace had died. He had been suffering from Parkinson's disease and was just 60 when he passed away in the Hampshire town of Basingstoke. After leaving Rangers in 1986 he had gone on to have spells with Seville in Spain as well as Colchester, with family ties in England, and returned to live in Spain following his retirement from management.

SUNDAY 25th JULY 1982

Hibs considered a £180,000 bid for their Scotland Under-21 defender Craig Paterson, lodged by Rangers boss John Greig. The 22-year-old was hot property and the Easter Road side were reluctant to let him go, but their Ibrox counterparts were determined and the player had already submitted a transfer request at the end of his Hibees contract. A £225,000 deal was eventually struck the following day, allowing Paterson to fly out to join his new team-mates for a pre-season tournament in France. He would go on to captain Rangers before moving to Motherwell and, post-football, carving out a successful career in broadcasting as an analyst with the BBC.

THURSDAY 26th JULY 2001

Rangers chairman David Murray made a chilling prediction as he stated he believed from eight to ten Scottish clubs would go to the wall within years. He claimed the balance sheets of that number of clubs demonstrated they were not viable businesses but insisted Rangers and Celtic were different because they had the ability to raise vast amounts of money from outside sources that the smaller clubs could only dream of. The owner could not have predicted that it would be his own club that would suffer most, with the liquidation process a decade down the line serving to highlight the point he himself had made about the precarious state of the national game's finances.

FRIDAY 27th JULY 1984

A young schoolboy-form signing became a fully fledged professional with Rangers, signing the paperwork to send himself on the way towards a long and distinguished career in the game. His name was Ian Durrant and, after being given his first contract by John Greig, within a year he made his first team debut under John Greig. Durrant starred in the midfield for Wallace and Graeme Souness, winning a succession of trophies and scoring cup final goals along the way. His horrendous knee injury at Aberdeen in 1988 stalled Durrant's career, but the diehard Ranger had the courage to battle back to fitness and reclaim his place in the team for more success in the 1990s. He moved to Kilmarnock in 1998 as a player and began a coaching career at Rugby Park that took him back to Ibrox, where he remains as part of Ally McCoist's backroom team.

SATURDAY 28th JULY 2012

The rebirth of Rangers took place as Ally McCoist took his new look newco team to Angus to face Brechin City in the Ramsdens Cup – a match televised live by BBC Alba and played in front of a sell out crowd of just over 4,000 at Glebe Park as the nation's attention focused on the first step on the road to recovery. Andrew Little made history as the first goal scorer in the new era with his early strike, although it took an injury time winner from veteran Lee McCulloch to clinch a 2-1 win. On 11th August at Balmoor Stadium the first Third Division fixture was played out in front of an intrigued mix of Rangers and Peterhead supporters, with McCoist's men held to a 2-2 draw.

WEDNESDAY 29th JULY 1992

It was fitting that Rangers provided the opposition for Inverness Caledonian stalwart Billy Urquhart's testimonial in the Highlands, with more than 6,000 turning out to pay tribute to the north star. Urquhart had two spells with Caley – with a stint at Ibrox sandwiched between. He was signed in a £15,000 deal from the Inverness club by John Greig in the summer of 1978 and won a League Cup medal in his first season at Rangers. With fierce competition for striking berths, he joined Wigan for £20,000 two years later and moved back to Caley the following year to resume his career in the Highland League.

SUNDAY 30th JULY 2006

The first competitive game under Paul Le Guen ended in a 2-1 win at Motherwell. New recruit Libor Sionko and Croatian star Dado Prso, who was made captain for the opening day of the season, both netted to give the Frenchman the perfect welcome gift. Le Guen said he was impressed with the good football his team played and the understanding between the players he had hastily knitted together during his summer rebuilding process. The cool and composed new coach spoke of his clear idea of the direction in which he was taking the club and appeared to be laying the foundations for a long stay in Glasgow. Those thoughts quickly evaporated as the dreams and plans began to unravel.

MONDAY 31st JULY 1967

The Ferguson family welcomed baby Derek into the world, the eldest of their two footballing sons. Just like his younger brother Barry would do, Derek impressed Rangers as a youngster and was snapped up for the Ibrox youth ranks. By the age of 21 he had been in the Gers' top team for five years and had been capped by Scotland, such was the impact he had made at the heart of the midfield under John Greig, Jock Wallace and Graeme Souness. Ferguson went on to win a hat-trick of League Cup winner's medals as well as a matching championship badge, before moving on to Hearts in a record breaking £750,000 move for the Tynecastle side in 1990. Ferguson also played for Sunderland and Falkirk, amongst others.

RANGERS
On This Day

AUGUST

FRIDAY 1st AUGUST 1986

Terry Butcher had emerged from the World Cup finals in the summer of 1986 as one of the most impressive defenders on view on the big stage. On this day he agreed his club future would rest in Scotland as the towering England stopper pledged his future to Rangers and committed to a £725,000 transfer from Ipswich that led to him taking on the Ibrox captaincy as he became the figurehead for the Graeme Souness revolution. Butcher was awarded a bumper four-year contract.

SATURDAY 1st AUGUST 1987

The new Edmiston Club opened its doors for the first time. Rangers Pools, the club's revenue generating arm, had ploughed £400,000 into the new look venue, occupying the former social club. The club was to be open to the 5,700 members of the Premier club and 6,000 pools agents, boasting a restaurant and three bars as well as a snooker room and function suite.

SATURDAY 2nd AUGUST 1890

The Rangers Sports became part and parcel of Ibrox life, with the annual meeting attracting star athletes from across the country for track and field events. By the time the 50th sports were held in 1942, there was a five-a-side element to what was primarily an athletics showcase. Back in the 19th century there was an 11-a-side competition attached to the event, with Rangers kicking off their Rangers Sports Trophy campaign on this day in 1890 with a 3-2 win against Linthouse. They went through to play Dumbarton a week later and triumphed 3-1 to collect the silverware.

THURSDAY 3rd AUGUST 1989

The first annual general meeting was staged after the furore surrounding the recruitment of Mo Johnston. Chairman David Murray and manager Graeme Souness faced a mixed reception as they met with shareholders, with a split in the room between those who welcomed the signing and those opposed to it. Souness and Murray each addressed a crowd of close to 2,000 and the manager said he was pleased with the support he had received from fans as he set about putting his stamp on every aspect of Ibrox life.

HAPPIER TIMES, BUT WHEN FORMER CELTIC STRIKER MO JOHNSTON FIRST ARRIVED IN AUGUST 1989, RANGERS FANS WERE SPLIT

THURSDAY 4th AUGUST 1966

British Railways announced that the 'football specials' carrying supporters from Glasgow Central to Ibrox Station were being discontinued. Rail chiefs pointed to a decreasing number of passengers as the reason, with 42,000 passengers carried in 1963/64 compared to the 20,000 who used the trains in 1965/66. The advent of supporters' club buses was blamed for the fall in train passenger numbers.

WEDNESDAY 4th AUGUST 1971

The first edition of *Rangers News* was piled on the newsstands as the club reached out to its supporters and bypassed the traditional media. The front page story for the historic publication was an interview with manager Willie Waddell in which he challenged his players to deliver the First Division championship in the new season. The publication was credited by the club as a means for keeping not just Ibrox diehards up to date with the latest happenings at the club but with keeping in touch with those exiled in England and abroad.

TUESDAY 4th AUGUST 1998

Bears knew Ally McCoist's career at Ibrox was over – but this was the day reality began to sink in as Kilmarnock announced they had agreed a one-year deal with the veteran striking star. Hibs had also been keen on landing the free agent while Queens Park Rangers expressed an interest, but he opted instead to follow his friend and former Gers team-mate Ian Durrant to Rugby Park. It was the same day on which Scotland captain Colin Hendry clinched his move to Rangers from Blackburn.

SUNDAY 5th AUGUST 1979

The Celtic Supporters Association called for the first Old Firm fixture of the season to be moved away from Ibrox – and received a flea in their ear from Rangers director Willie Waddell. The Parkhead fans claimed to be concerned about segregation arrangements for the match, with Ibrox in the midst of reconstruction to make it a 42,000-seat stadium. Waddell blasted the claims from the Celtic association and insisted Ibrox was fit and able to host the match. It went ahead as planned on 18th August, ending in a 2-2 draw.

THURSDAY 6th AUGUST 1987

Trevor Francis signed the contract that took him from Italian side Atalanta to the chillier climes of Govan as he became a Rangers player and answered a call from friend Graeme Souness. Negotiations had been protracted but a £75,000 fee was agreed with the continental club and the 33-year-old England legend settled on a pay-as-you-play deal due to injury problems which had restricted his appearances in previous seasons, aiming to avoid accusations that he had landed in Scotland for one last pay day.

FRIDAY 7th AUGUST 1987

Graeme Souness and Walter Smith received an extra bonus for their efforts in leading the club to the Premier Division championship in their first season together at Ibrox. The pair were paraded in front of the media to collect keys to gleaming new cars presented by chief executive David Holmes, with Souness gifted the use of a Daimler and Smith picking up the keys to a new Jaguar. After making the presentation, Holmes departed the press call in an Austin Metro.

MONDAY 8th AUGUST 1977

It was announced that the Rangers Social Club had closed its doors for good. Despite having 11,000 members, the club had fallen on hard times and was reported to be carrying debts of up to £180,000 and the £4 annual subscription was not enough to make it a viable concern. The entertainment venue had opened in 1971 in an Ibrox building leased from Rangers.

SATURDAY 9th AUGUST 1986

Graeme Souness led Rangers into competitive action for the first time, but Hibs had not read the script as the high profile new boss made his eagerly anticipated debut as a manager and on the pitch as part of his new-look Rangers side. Hibs won the explosive match at Easter Road 2-1 and Souness was sent off for a brutal challenge on George McCluskey as he played his first ever club match in the Scottish top flight. He later apologised for the tackle that saw him take an early bath but also stated he wanted his team to stand up for themselves in the season ahead.

WEDNESDAY 9th AUGUST 1995

Paul Gascoigne made his eagerly-awaited competitive debut for Rangers when Anorthosis Famagusta arrived in Glasgow on Champions League qualifying duty. The game ended 1-0 to the hosts and the Gazza show was officially off and running after his high profile £4.3m move from Italian side Lazio that summer and even higher profile pre-season campaign – including his impromptu flute mime. The Englishman put fears of his injury problems behind him as he established himself as a mainstay of Walter Smith's side.

FRIDAY 10th AUGUST 2007

David Murray made a pledge to fans that he would conduct a 'fit and proper person' test on the next owner of Rangers, as the supremo prepared to step away from his club. He also revealed that he would not rule out the possibility of a foreign owner taking control, insisting he would judge all approaches on their merits rather than the nationality of the suitor. Murray asked Rangers fans to "trust" him to pick the right person to sell to.

FRIDAY 11th AUGUST 2000

Rangers signalled a warning to the rest of the Scottish game when the club revealed an agreement in principle had been reached on the idea of a pan-European league. David Murray had travelled to Amsterdam for talks and had been joined by a representative from Celtic. Led by the Dutch sides Ajax, PSV and Feyenoord, the so-called Atlantic League would feature teams from Scotland, the Netherlands, Belgium, Portugal and Scandinavia. Despite early optimism, the scheme failed to reach fruition.

THURSDAY 12th AUGUST 2010

Former England striker James Beattie arrived in Glasgow to put the finishing touches to the deal that took him to Ibrox from Stoke City. The 32-year-old agreed a two-year contract, following hard on the heels of the news that veteran midfielder Lee McCulloch had signed a contract extension. The reliance on the seasoned campaigners hinted at the restrictions manager Walter Smith was working under as the new season loomed, with the boss admitting he had been frustrated by his inability to make significant reinforcements.

SATURDAY 13th AUGUST 1960

A crowd of 51,000 crammed in to Ibrox to see Jim Baxter run out and make his debut. It should have been a low key game, a League Cup encounter with Partick Thistle, but Slim Jim's presence livened up the occasion. Baxter, who wore the number ten shirt rather than his more familiar number six, played his part in a 3-1 win as Jimmy Millar's double and Alex Scott's goal eased Scot Symon's side into gear as 1960/61 kicked off.

SATURDAY 13th AUGUST 1988

When Rangers ran out to face Hamilton at Douglas Park they could never have imagined what the club was embarking upon. The relatively unremarkable victory against the Accies, with Gary Stevens and Ally McCoist on target, was the first game in what became the run to nine-in-a-row. For the record, the team that took to the park on that Saturday afternoon was: Chris Woods, Gary Stevens, Stuart Munro, Richard Gough, Ray Wilkins, Kevin Drinkell, John Brown, Ally McCoist, Ian Durrant and Mark Walters, with substitute appearances from Derek Ferguson and Davie Cooper.

SUNDAY 14th AUGUST 2011

Rangers rejected a £700,000 bid from Bolton for promising young winger Gregg Wylde. Owen Coyle was keen to recruit the Scotland Under-21 star but was given short shrift by Ibrox chiefs. Bolton eventually got his man in March the following year and signed Wylde without a fee, with the player a free agent after taking voluntary redundancy when Rangers entered administration. Wylde agreed a bumper three-year contract with the Trotters.

TUESDAY 15th AUGUST 1933

It was a case of close but no cigar as Rangers went close to matching the ten-goal margin that would have equalled the club's best ever league win. Bill Struth's side fell just two short when they welcomed Ayr United to Ibrox and duly battered them with a nine-goal barrage, led by Alex Smith with his double hat-trick. Alex Stevenson managed a treble himself, although the Honest Men did have the consolation of a single goal.

SATURDAY 15th AUGUST 1981

The group stage of the League Cup threw up some mismatches along the way and the 1981/82 season was no different, with Raith Rovers crushed 8-1 by an impressive looking Rangers side at Ibrox. Ian Redford scored four against the hapless Fife side while Bobby Russell scored a double, Sandy Jardine and Colin McAdam also joined the early season party at the start of what proved to be a winning campaign.

SATURDAY 16th AUGUST 1890

A crowd of 3,400 inquisitive souls turned out to watch a major milestone in the history of the fledgling Rangers Football Club. On this day the emerging team faced Hearts in their first ever Scottish Football League fixture and they signalled their intentions for the landmark season with an impressive 5-2 victory. Kerr had the honour of scoring the first league goal and grabbed another on the day, joining McCreadie and James McPherson on the score sheet. The Jambos scored an own goal to round things off.

WEDNESDAY 17th AUGUST 1966

Jim Forrest went goal crazy as he tormented Stirling Albion at Anfield in the League Cup group stages. The up and coming young striker hit five for Scot Symon's side as they demolished their First Division rivals 8-0 to signal their intentions for the season. George McLean added a double while Davy Wilson also scored against the dispirited Binos.

WEDNESDAY 18th AUGUST 1971

Rangers demolished Ayr United 4-0 at Ibrox – but manager Willie Waddell was not a happy man. It was not his own team that Waddell was angry with, his fury reserved instead for Ayr and their manager Ally MacLeod. Waddell criticised the Honest Men for their negative tactics and warned that the type of defensive display Ayr produced would be enough to lead the paying public to keep their wallets in their pockets and turn their backs on the Scottish game. MacLeod insisted he had not sent his team out to frustrate their hosts and that injury had weakened his options in attack.

TUESDAY 19th AUGUST 1986

The SFA threw the book at Rangers as the club and Graeme Souness faced officials in a hearing to consider the fall-out from the violent scenes in the opening game of the season against Hibs, when the player-manager was red carded for his involvement. Souness was banned for three matches while the club was hit with a £5,000 fine. Hibs were fined £1,000 for their part in the tempestuous afternoon while 21 of the 22 players on the park had two points added to their disciplinary record. Only Hibs keeper Alan Rough escaped the punishment – but he already had points winging his way after being booked during the stormy encounter.

SATURDAY 20th AUGUST 1983

New recruit Ally McCoist pulled on the famous jersey for the first time in a competitive game as John Greig's new-look Rangers side tackled St Mirren at Ibrox in the opening game of the 1983/84 season. McCoist did not wear the number nine shirt that became his trademark, instead that went to his new strike partner Sandy Clark and the rookie was handed number eight. The duo had been paired together as room-mates by the manager during pre-season in a bid to enable the new boy to benefit from the experience of Clark. McCoist, recruited from Sunderland, endured a slow start to his Ibrox career but went on to become a hero with his natural ability in front of goal.

WEDNESDAY 21st AUGUST 1974

For the first and only time, Rangers kicked off a match on one day and finished it on another. Their tie against Barcelona at the Nou Camp in the Trofeo Juan Gamper challenge tournament did not start until 10.45pm, with the third and fourth place play-off in the four-team event preceding it. The late start did not do the visitors any favours, with Barca running out 4-1 winners. Graham Fyfe scored the consolation goal for the Gers – just a day after being singled out by Barcelona star Johan Cruyff for his performance against Athletic Bilbao in the opening game of the mini-tournament. Sandy Jardine, who scored the only goal of the game against Bilbao, was the other player picked out by Cruyff for special mention.

MONDAY 22nd AUGUST 2011

New signing Carlos Bocanegra was granted a visa to enter the country, allowing him to join his team-mates for training for the first time. The USA captain had already played for the club, having made his debut in a European tie against Maribor the previous week, but had been unable to travel to Glasgow due to the paperwork delay.

SATURDAY 23rd AUGUST 1997

Dundee United were lambs to the slaughter as Marco Negri scented blood at Ibrox. The Italian, who had scored two against Hearts on his debut earlier in the month, banged home five goals against the Arabs to strike fear into the hearts of defenders up and down the country. The deadly forward had arrived from Perugia that summer and the £3.7m investment looked to be the deal of the decade.

FRIDAY 24th AUGUST 1990

Terry Hurlock signed from Millwall. The Londoner had been a cult figure with the Lions and previous club Brentford, earning similar status at Ibrox with his rugged style ... and permed hair. Graeme Souness recruited the midfield enforcer, who went on to win a B cap with England as well as winning the Premier Division title and Scottish Cup in his sole campaign as a Gers player. Hurlock also collected a pile of yellow and red cards and, with the dubious honour of the worst disciplinary record in a single season by any player in the Scottish game, left to ply his trade with Southampton.

FRIDAY 25th AUGUST 2006

Paul Le Guen got it right on this day, a rare occasion in Rangers history. Austria Vienna confirmed that the French coach had been in touch in a bid to secure the services of £1m-rated Bosnian defender Sasa Papac. The 26-year-old was granted permission to talk to le Guen and agreed terms to make the switch to the SPL, following Vienna team-mates Filip Sebo and Libor Sionko to Glasgow. Whilst the other two were soon surplus to requirements, Papac remained in place and became one of the first names on the Rangers teamsheet.

MONDAY 26th AUGUST 1918

The London Gazette had some rare Rangers interest on this day as former Rangers player Finlay Speedie was listed as a recipient of the Military Medal. Speedie, by that time plying his trade with Dumbarton, was fighting in World War One. He had joined the Argyll and Sutherland Highlanders to play his part in the Great War and received his medal for courage in the field during a fierce spell of fighting on the Western Front.

WEDNESDAY 26th AUGUST 2009

David Murray announced his decision to step down from the chairman's role for a second and final time. On this occasion the club owner was replaced by Alastair Johnston, who had served as a director for five years up to that point. Murray insisted the move, which included resigning from the board, had not been influenced by the banks and reflected on his greatest memories from two stints as chairman.

TUESDAY 27th AUGUST 1985

History was made as STV announced plans to broadcast the first ever live televised Scottish league match. Not surprisingly the TV firm chose an Old Firm clash – but the date angered both clubs, with the media chiefs dictating a Sunday match on 17th November 1985. Rangers and Celtic were uncomfortable with the idea of having their fixture schedule determined by television executives, little realising that it would be a sign of things to come as future broadcast deals saw kick-off times and dates shuffled to suit the TV schedules.

WEDNESDAY 28th AUGUST 1946

War was over and football was returning to some semblance of normality, with Rangers setting out their stall early in the campaign with a thumping 8-1 victory at Ibrox against Third Lanark. Both Willie Thornton and Jimmy Caskie scored trebles while Torry Gillick and Jimmy Duncanson played the supporting roles with their goals. The hat-trick proved to be Caskie's only goals of the season. Rangers went on to win the title while Thirds regrouped to challenge for a place in the top half of the table.

TUESDAY 28th AUGUST 1962

This was the day future manager Walter Smith was banned from Ibrox – for his own good. Scot Symon, boss at the time, wrote to Smith's father to deny a request for the youngster to be allowed to watch Rangers matches from the Ibrox track. The correspondence came after Smith broke a leg playing football and his dad sought a way to enable him to continue taking his boy to watch his heroes. Symon told the Smiths that the police would not approve and that the young fan would also be at risk of being hit by the ball.

TUESDAY 29th AUGUST 2000

When Michael Mols scored the opener against Glentoran with a classic left-foot strike it represented more than simply a goal in a friendly. It was the completion of the Dutch striker's rehabilitation after a horrendous knee injury in November 1999. Mols had been sidelined for the best part of a season but was back with a bang as his side defeated their Irish visitors 3-0 at Ibrox. Rod Wallace and Alan Johnston also scored.

SATURDAY 30th AUGUST 1975

A brave new era for Scottish football began as the Premier Division kicked off in earnest. The ten-club top flight launched in dramatic fashion, with an Old Firm encounter providing the highlight of the opening weekend's action. Celtic travelled to Ibrox and were defeated 2-1 as Derek Johnstone earned the distinction of scoring the first Premier Division goal for Rangers. Quinton Young was the other man on target for the hosts.

WEDNESDAY 30th AUGUST 2000

Hundreds of Bears gathered outside Ibrox to welcome new recruit Ronald de Boer. The £4.5m capture of the Barcelona star represented a huge coup for the club and Dick Advocaat, who revealed a lengthy pursuit of the Netherlands hero. He had worked with the midfielder during his time as coach to the Dutch national team and backed him to be a huge hit in Scotland. The following day, striker John Hartson failed the medical he hoped would clinch his switch from Wimbledon to Ibrox.

WEDNESDAY 31st AUGUST 1983

Ally McCoist broke his duck with Rangers as he scored his first goal for the club in a 4-0 League Cup victory over Clydebank at Ibrox. Like buses, McCoist goals seldom came on their own and after whetting his appetite he added another in the same game to get off and running. Few of the 8,500 who witnessed his first goals in Light Blue could have predicted they were watching the start of something extra special as the fresh-faced young striker embarked on his incredible run of scoring exploits.

THURSDAY 31st AUGUST 2006

A rare thing happened on this day – Paul Le Guen signed a player who made a lasting contribution to the Ibrox cause. Sasa Papac agreed his move to Ibrox from Austria Vienna and the £450,000 investment in the versatile Bosnian defender proved to be the shrewdest piece of business conducted by the French boss during his brief tenure in the Rangers manager's office as the player went on to prove a dependable and capable part of the squad under le Guen, Walter Smith and Ally McCoist.

RANGERS
On This Day

SEPTEMBER

WEDNESDAY 1st SEPTEMBER 2004

David Murray returned to the top job when he was confirmed as chairman after days of speculation. He resumed control having handed over to John McClelland two years previously, with McClelland stepping back to become vice-chairman after the latest reshuffle. It came shortly after Murray had bought the 20 per cent stake in the club held by ENIC at a cost of £8.7m and taken his own shareholding to more than 86 per cent.

SATURDAY 2nd SEPTEMBER 1939

Rangers retained their place at the head of the First Division with a 2-2 win at Third Lanark – but it proved the final game of that truncated league season. The competition was abandoned after that round of games as, the following day, Britain and France declared war on Germany and sport was put well and truly on the back burner. In place of the top flight competition, a regional league was put in place for the remainder of that campaign and Rangers came out on top in the Western Division, with Queen of the South second.

SATURDAY 2nd SEPTEMBER 1961

Scot Symon blooded a young player named John Greig as his side entertained Airdrie at Ibrox in the League Cup group stages. Greig did not look out of place among the big boys, despite his lack of experience, and helped his new team-mates to a 4-1 victory by scoring one of the goals. It was the first of 14 appearances he made in the 1961/62 season in all competitions as he was eased into the first team fold.

MONDAY 3rd SEPTEMBER 1973

Rangers trainer Stan Anderson swapped Ibrox for Shawfield, as he settled into his new job as manager of Clyde. Anderson had left the security of his role on the backroom team under Willie Waddell and then Jock Wallace to embrace the opportunity to be his own man with the Bully Wee. He pledged to bring a Rangers-style work ethic and attention to detail with his to his new club, noting that his charges had room for improvement when it came to fitness but praising them for their football ability.

WEDNESDAY 4th SEPTEMBER 1935

Rangers kicked-off a mini-series against English opposition with a 1-1 draw south of the border against Sheffield Wednesday. The Owls made the return trip two weeks later, when they were beaten 2-0 at Ibrox, while Arsenal were also visitors to Govan that month. The Gunners held their hosts to a 2-2 draw in a match that had captured the imagination of the paying public, with both home games against the English clubs drawing crowds in the region of 30,000 – far in excess of the average league gate that season.

WEDNESDAY 5th SEPTEMBER 1962

A 4-0 victory over Seville in the opening round of the 1962/63 European Cup Winners' Cup at Ibrox on this day appeared to make the return leg in Spain three weeks later a mere formality. However, the 26th September encounter proved to be a battle of proportions Rangers had never seen before and have never seen since as the Spaniards, their pride hurt by the Ibrox thumping, set about brutally exacting their revenge. Seville won 2-0 on the night but football was a side show as running battles all over the pitch ensued.

FRIDAY 6th SEPTEMBER 1935

A plaque on the wall of a community centre in East Lothian marks an important date in Rangers' history. It was on this day in the village of Wallyford that Jock Wallace was born, often making the trip from his home as a young boy to go and watch Rangers when they visited Edinburgh. As well as the plaque in his home village, there are also two roads named after the former Rangers boss in his home village: Wallace Avenue and Wallace Crescent.

FRIDAY 7th SEPTEMBER 2001

It was confirmed that Billy Dodds had retired from international football. The Rangers striker had informed Craig Brown of his decision following a 2-0 defeat against Belgium in the World Cup qualifiers two days earlier, but the decision was not confirmed until later. Dodds had played 26 times for his country and scored seven goals, but decided to call time on his duty with the national side.

TUESDAY 8th SEPTEMBER 1992

Far-flung friendlies are nothing new, but this 1992 trip was slightly different. Rather than exotic opposition in an exotic location, the logistical nightmare was a venture to deepest Devon to face minnows Exeter City in front of just 2,000 people. Walter Smith sent a decent squad for the game, with his side recording a 1-1 draw thanks to Dale Gordon's goal. The match had been arranged as part of the package that had taken Chris Vinnicombe from Exeter to Rangers three years earlier, a sweetener to enable the deal to go through.

SATURDAY 9th SEPTEMBER 2006

The Bill Struth Stand was officially unveiled before the SPL match against Falkirk at Ibrox. The Main Stand had been given the new name as a tribute to the legendary manager, with the launch coming a fortnight before the 50th anniversary of his death. The previous year a bronze bust of Struth had been unveiled on the main staircase as the club sought to maintain the memory of the man who was behind so much of the club's success on and off the pitch.

MONDAY 10th SEPTEMBER 1979

Davie Cooper had plenty to celebrate. He was told by Scotland manager Jock Stein that he had been picked to win his first cap, named in the side to tackle Peru two days later, and was also crowned Scottish football's personality of the month – winning a giant bottle of whisky with which he could toast his double achievement. Cooper was joined in the side to face Peru by Ibrox colleague Sandy Jardine.

FRIDAY 11th SEPTEMBER 1942

A baby was born in Edinburgh and his name was John Greig. He would grow up in the capital city as a Hearts fan but it was Rangers who spotted his potential as a schoolboy and lured him as a teenager from east coast to west to start a long association with Ibrox. Greig always remained true to his Edinburgh roots and lived in the city throughout his playing days, only relocating closer to Glasgow when he was appointed manager.

DAVIE COOPER PICKED UP HIS FIRST SCOTLAND CAP IN SEPTEMBER 1979

SATURDAY 11th SEPTEMBER 1886

Govan stood between Rangers and a place in the second round of the Scottish Cup in 1886/87 but the Clydeside outfit were no match for their opponents, falling to a 9-1 defeat. The Gers went on to beat Westbourne 5-2 in the second round but went out at the next stage when they fell 2-0 to Cambuslang.

TUESDAY 11th SEPTEMBER 1979

Sandy Jardine was named Scotland captain by national boss Jock Stein as he prepared his side to face Peru in a friendly at Hampden. The Rangers stalwart, a veteran of two World Cup campaigns, had fallen out of favour under Ally MacLeod but was restored to the team by Stein and was a surprise choice for the skipper's role. Kenny Dalglish had been tipped for the job.

MONDAY 12th SEPTEMBER 2011

Owner Craig Whyte admitted there were "challenges ahead" for Rangers, but claimed there was no threat to the club's existence. Whyte was on the defensive after reports of cash woes intensified, but he was adamant Rangers would be around long after he was "dead and buried" and insisted the tax cases would not force his hand.

THURSDAY 13th SEPTEMBER 1984

The appearance of the Rangers team changed for all-time as double glazing firm CR Smith announced they had clinched a shirt sponsorship deal that would see their name emblazoned on the kits of both Rangers and Celtic. The joint agreement was reported to be worth £500,000 and was masterminded by the firm's managing director Gerard Eadie – who said his football loyalties lay in the less glamorous surroundings of Central Park, Cowdenbeath, as Blue Brazil fan. The addition of the brand to the front of the Umbro kit represented the first time a sponsor had appeared on the Rangers jersey – a concept fully embraced in the years that followed, with the exception of 2012/13 when Tennent's accepted a smaller display as part of the switch to a retro design to coincide with the 40th anniversary of the European Cup Winners' Cup success.

TUESDAY 14th SEPTEMBER 2004

Chairman David Murray announced a share issue designed to raise £57m and tackle the club's debt. Murray revealed he and his company would underwrite £50m of the total as he attempted to address the £72m deficit. It came at a time when he announced a £5.9m loss for the latest financial year. It represented a big improvement on the previous 12 months – when the club suffered a £29.6m hit.

WEDNESDAY 15th SEPTEMBER 1971

The first game in the run to success in the 1971/72 European Cup Winners' Cup took place in France as Rangers travelled to face Stade Rennes and returned with a 1-1 draw thanks to Willie Johnston's goal after a determined and resilient display. The first-round tie was completed 13 days later when Alex MacDonald scored the only goal of the second leg at Ibrox and ensured safe passage at the start of the momentous journey that would end in Barcelona.

THURSDAY 16th FEBRUARY 1993

Future Australian captain Craig Moore became a fully fledged professional with Rangers, having been snapped up as a teenage member of his country's famed institute of sport. Moore rose to become Rangers skipper and made more than 200 appearances over 12 years at Ibrox, with a short stint with Crystal Palace in the 1998/99 season sandwiched in the middle, before sampling German football with Borussia Monchengladbach in 2005. Moore also had two years with Newcastle United before returning to Australia to wind down his career.

SATURDAY 17th SEPTEMBER 1955

The League Cup quarter-finals were still played over two legs when Hamilton were paired with Rangers in the 1955/56 season and the Accies gave themselves a chance of upsetting the apple cart when they restricted their more illustrious opponents to a 2-1 scoreline at Douglas Park. It proved to be a false sense of optimism as the Lanarkshire side were thumped 8-0 in the return game on 17th September at Ibrox, with Alex Scott's hat-trick and doubles from Billy Simpson and Johnny Hubbard joined by a goal from John Prentice.

TUESDAY 18th SEPTEMBER 1917

King George V arrived in Glasgow and Ibrox was his destination. The monarch was greeted by tens of thousands inside the stadium, with the public turning out to witness an open air investiture ceremony. There was another royal visit on 3rd May 1938 when King George VI and Queen Elizabeth formally opened the Glasgow Empire Exhibition, which was being staged nearby at Bellahouston Park.

TUESDAY 18th SEPTEMBER 2001

Rangers were spared a trip into troubled Dagestan when Uefa ruled in favour of common sense on this day. The players and managers had been reluctant to travel to face Anzi Makhachkala due to a spate of bombings and terror attacks. Eventually Uefa admitted it had made a mistake in its refusal to agree to a switch of location and agreed with Rangers that the tie should be played elsewhere and chose Poland as the neutral venue. Captain Barry Ferguson was among the most outspoken about the situation, insisting he would not put his life in jeopardy for the sake of a football match.

MONDAY 19th SEPTEMBER 1927

Recent changes to the Scottish Cup format have given junior players the length and breadth of the country the dream of locking horns with top-flight sides. On this day in 1927 a group of juniors got that opportunity when an East of Scotland select picked from that grade tackled mighty Rangers at Tynecastle. The juniors, not surprisingly, were overwhelmed by their senior counterparts and fell to a 7-2 defeat as Jimmy Marshall banged in four for the west coast side.

SATURDAY 20th SEPTEMBER 1980

Hopes of a Rangers resurgence after a trophyless season in 1979/80 were boosted early in the following campaign when Kilmarnock were annihilated at Rugby Park as part of an unbeaten run at the start of the term. Killie were thumped 8-1 by John Greig's rampant side, with John McDonald's hat-trick and a double from Ian Redford the highlights. Colin McAdam, Sandy Jardine and young Jim Bett were the others on target as the Gers made it six without defeat in the Premier Division.

TUESDAY 21st SEPTEMBER 1926

The European Cup Winners' Cup, the SPL trophy, the Scottish Cup, the League Cup, all hold a special place on the Ibrox roll of honour. Less well known is the Hospital Challenge Cup, a piece of silverware collected in the 1920s when the Gers ventured south and tackled Huddersfield Town in front of 15,000 people. Rangers won the day, clinching a 2-1 victory through George Henderson and Alan Morton.

TUESDAY 22nd SEPTEMBER 1925

A true giant of Ibrox was given a boost. Davie Meiklejohn was the subject of a benefit match at Ibrox, with Huddersfield Town providing the opposition and winning 2-1. It came six years after the captain had first appeared in a blue jersey, with the cool and calm defender going on to make more than 550 appearances between 1919 and 1936 as well as picking up an impressive collection of medals. He was capped 15 times by Scotland.

TUESDAY 23rd SEPTEMBER 1958

In Dundee a future Rangers player was born, with Davie Dodds making his most important debut. Dodds goes down in history as one of the more unlikely Ibrox heroes, but he had an important role to play among the big money buys during the Graeme Souness era. He was recruited as striking cover after Gary McSwegan broke a leg in the 1989/90 season, costing £125,000 from Aberdeen after arriving at Pittodrie via his first club Dundee United and Swiss outfit Neuchatel. He was 32 but young enough to spend two seasons in and around the first team, retiring in 1991 and winning a place on the coaching staff.

MONDAY 24th SEPTEMBER 1962

A star was born as a certain Alistair Murdoch McCoist made his entrance to the world in Bellshill. McCoist would grow up in East Kilbride and cut his footballing teeth with the Calderwood Blue Star Boys' Club before venturing into professional football as a youngster with St Johnstone. His home town has never forgotten its most favourite son, with a £3.5m sports centre in East Kilbride unveiled in 2009 named in honour of McCoist.

TUESDAY 25th SEPTEMBER 1979

Scottish football was greeted with the shock news that Willie Waddell had quit his role as general manager of Rangers. The Ibrox veteran retained his place on the board of directors but said he needed a break from the pressure of his day to day responsibilities at the club, having taken on the position following his decision to hand over team affairs to Jock Wallace in 1972. The recently appointed secretary Campbell Ogilvie, a man who would become a key figure in the years that followed, was tipped to take on the administration burden.

SATURDAY 26th SEPTEMBER 1987

Morton had a miserable return to the Premier Division in the 1987/88 season, falling straight back through the relegation trapdoor after winning just three of their 44 fixtures back in the top flight. Rangers did nothing to ease their pain when they met on this day, putting seven past the Cappielow side at Ibrox without reply. Ally McCoist and Mark Falco were left to fight for the match ball after each notched a hat-trick, with Robert Fleck also on target.

MONDAY 27th SEPTEMBER 2010

The SFA confirmed former Rangers captain Barry Ferguson's career with Scotland had ended. Ferguson was banished from the international scene while still at Ibrox, punished in 2009 for breaches in discipline including a drinking session during George Burley's squad's stay at Cameron House and then the infamous V-sign gesture at cameras days later. Ferguson later moved from Rangers to Birmingham and it was while he was with the English club that he rejected an approach from new manager Craig Levein to consider a return to the Hampden fold, news announced by the SFA.

THURSDAY 28th SEPTEMBER 1889

Kelvinside provided the opposition in a Scottish Cup first-round derby that attracted 2,000 enthusiastic fans. The result fell emphatically in favour of Rangers, who scored 13 without reply on a memorable afternoon for the burgeoning club. The campaign was cut short in the third round when Vale of Leven knocked them out after a replay.

FORMER RANGERS AND SCOTLAND SKIPPER BARRY FERGUSON LEARNED HIS INTERNATIONAL CAREER WAS ENDED IN SEPTEMBER 2010

FRIDAY 29th SEPTEMBER 1939

In the Fife mining village of Hill of Beath a bouncing baby boy by the name of Jim Baxter was born. Baxter would go on to become a star on the world stage, but it was in the east of the country that he made his way in life. Baxter served as a coal miner while he juggled football commitments with work life in his early years, starring for junior outfit Crossgates Primrose before being spotted by Raith Rovers and given a place in the senior game.

MONDAY 29th SEPTEMBER 1986

Phil Boersma became the final piece in the Graeme Souness coaching jigsaw. The former Liverpool squad man, who had been a midfielder with the Reds and Middlesbrough in the 1970s, was a man the Ibrox gaffer knew well and was handed the role of trainer-coach. Boersma, who had been assistant manager at Lincoln City, doubled as physiotherapist during his time at Rangers and followed his boss to Liverpool and subsequent clubs as one of his most trusted lieutenants.

WEDNESDAY 30th SEPTEMBER 1908

Glamour friendlies have become the preserve of testimonials in modern football, boosting the bank balances of a string of rich and famous stars of the game. In the early days of the club those fixtures were used for more earthy causes, with Rangers tackling Newcastle United at St James' Park on this day in aid of the Unemployed Relief Fund. The Toon travelled north for a return match at Ibrox the following week, winning both matches and scoring four in each. Rangers replied with a single goal in Newcastle and two of their own in Glasgow.

RANGERS
On This Day

OCTOBER

THURSDAY 1st OCTOBER 1998

Rino Gattuso was not a renowned scorer but his effort against Israeli side Beitar Jerusalem was worthy of note. It took the Italian midfielder just 20 seconds to score against the visitors at Ibrox when they met in the Uefa Cup on the back of a 1-1 draw in Israel. The Gers went on to win the game 4-2.

SATURDAY 2nd OCTOBER 1954

Scot Symon became an East Fife legend as a cup-winning manager with the Methil men – but he was in no mood to do his old side any favours when he returned to Bayview as boss of Rangers on this day. His charges ran out 7-2 winners thanks to doubles from Derek Grierson and Willie Paton while Willie Gardiner and Willie McCulloch scored to add to George Young's penalty goal. It proved not to be a lucky omen, with Symon's team having to settle for third place behind Aberdeen and Celtic in the 1954/55 league season.

FRIDAY 2nd OCTOBER 1987

Richard Gough became Scottish football's first £1m man as he clinched his dream move to Rangers from Tottenham. The Spurs skipper had first been targeted more than a year previously, when Graeme Souness attempted to make Gough his first signing for the club. On this day the deal was clinched and the dominant central defender was at Ibrox to complete the switch – and take the Souness spending spree past £4m in total. Gough had been at Ibrox eight years previously for a trial during John Greig's reign as manager, but was rejected.

MONDAY 3rd OCTOBER 2011

Rangers midfielder Matt McKay was crowned Australia's footballer of the year. The former Brisbane Roar man had struggled to make an impact at Ibrox following his move to Scotland, but clearly had made a lasting impression on players in his homeland. His fellow professionals voted for him ahead of AZ Alkmaar playmaker Brett Holman and Everton star Tim Cahill. McKay received his award from former Gers hero Craig Moore during an awards dinner in Sydney.

SATURDAY 4th OCTOBER 1958

The tone for the 1958/59 season was set early as, just half a dozen games into the First Division campaign, Rangers met Dunfermline at East End Park. The match ended 7-1 in favour of the visitors as Scot Symon's team embarked on a run that would take them all the way to the championship and the hosts set off on a season that would see them successfully battle against relegation from the top division. Johnny Hubbard, with his hat-trick, was the star man but Ralph Brand, Sammy Baird, George Duncan and Alex Scott were also on target.

TUESDAY 5th OCTOBER 1954

Rangers cantered to victory against a British Army select side at Ibrox in a match that tempted more than 30,000 people through the turnstiles. The quality was poor, by all accounts, but the result was satisfying as the Gers ran out 3-0 winners in one of a series of matches against the Army during the 1950s. Derek Grierson, with a double, and Willie Waddell, with a stunning long range free-kick, were on target.

WEDNESDAY 6th OCTOBER 1965

George McLean was the hero of the hour and a half as he helped his side to victory in a pulsating League Cup semi-final at Hampden. Kilmarnock put up a stiff fight but were beaten 6-4 in an incredible tie packed with goals and excitement at both ends. McLean's hat-trick, including a goal from the penalty spot, was the highlight of a game that also featured goals from Alex Willoughby, Jim Forrest and Willie Henderson. McLean's goals took his tally for the competition to nine in just five appearances.

TUESDAY 7th OCTOBER 1997

More than 4,300 crammed into the scenic Caledonian Stadium on the shores of the Moray Firth as Scotland's newest club, Inverness Caledonian Thistle, officially opened their first permanent home. Rangers were the invited guests for the occasion and did their best to spoil the big day, winning 4-3 with a double from Peter van Vossen and further goals from Alex Cleland and Stalle Setnsaas.

THURSDAY 8th OCTOBER 2009

Chief executive Martin Bain made the bold prediction that Rangers would leave the SPL within a decade. The Ibrox supremo spoke of his frustration that lowly top-flight clubs south of the border could earn 15 times the amount of the revenue from television rights and sponsorship than the Old Firm could while playing in Scotland. The prospect of an Atlantic League, involving clubs from a string of European divisions, reared its head again.

SATURDAY 9th OCTOBER 1976

The demon drink was blamed for ugly scenes in Birmingham as a friendly against Aston Villa was abandoned due to crowd trouble. There were 25,000 inside Villa Park and a large portion had travelled down from Glasgow for the game. Trouble broke out after the hosts went 2-0 up, with cans and bottles raining down on the pitch and violence in the stands as police attempted to restore order. The referee abandoned the game with more than 35 minutes left with Villa officials blaming heavy drinking among Rangers fans, including on supporters' buses, for the problems.

THURSDAY 10th OCTOBER 2002

Rangers faced a goalkeeping crisis after a training ground clash. Allan McGregor, back-up keeper to Stefan Klos at that point, was hospitalised with concussion after a collision with Sunderland striker Kevin Kyle during a Scotland Under-21 session. The news from the young Scots' preparations for a trip to Iceland was particularly worrying for Alex McLeish, who had sent his other senior shot stopper, Jesper Christiansen, on loan to German side Wolfsburg.

TUESDAY 11th OCTOBER 1988

Graeme Souness made the first play in David Murray's takeover bid as the manager, a close friend of Murray, approached chairman David Holmes to float the idea. Souness, who was ready to plough some of his own wealth into the deal to buy the club, was encouraged by the response and within ten days news had filtered back from Holmes that club owner Lawrence Marlborough was prepared to sell if the price was right. The plans had been kept under wraps but behind the scenes things were beginning to take shape.

THURSDAY 11th OCTOBER 2001

A deal with software developer Akaei was announced that would see the club branch into the video game sector for the first time. The deal, believed to be worth six figures to the Ibrox board, paved the way for the English firm to create the management game *Rangers Football Coach* for the PC after collating precise information on the playing and behavioural characteristics of every member of the playing staff – enabling fans to try their hand at leading the Light Blues from the comfort of their own desks.

MONDAY 12th OCTOBER 1987

Ian Durrant declared himself fit and available for Scotland as he linked up with the international squad ahead of the European Championship qualifier against Belgium at Hampden. Durrant had stunned Rangers days earlier by requesting a transfer, which had been granted by Graeme Souness. Durrant insisted the turmoil at club level would not have an impact on his ability to perform for Scotland and said his mind was fully focussed on the task facing Andy Roxburgh's side.

MONDAY 13th OCTOBER 1980

The Anglo-Scottish Cup's short-lived existence ended in the 1980/81 season, with the summer tournament between teams from north and south of the border struggling to capture the imagination after its introduction in the 1970s. On this day Rangers welcomed Chesterfield to Ibrox in the quarter-final and drew 1-1, with Gordon Dalziel on target, before travelling south 15 days later and losing 3-0 to crash out. Chesterfield went on to win the competition and become the last name engraved on the silverware.

FRIDAY 14th OCTOBER 1983

Rangers confirmed they would send a team to compete in the new Tennent's Sixes competition, due to launch in 1984. Aberdeen were the only top-flight side to reject the idea, not tempted by the £3,000 appearance fee or the lure of a £5,000 first prize. The six-a-side event, to be staged in Falkirk, would see Rangers among the seeded teams and was full endorsed by the SFA in a bid to give a fresh impetus to the Scottish game.

WEDNESDAY 15th OCTOBER 2008

Football was put in perspective when it was announced the looming fixture against Dundee United had been postponed as a mark of respect for Arabs chairman Eddie Thompson, who had died that morning. The SPL had the full support of Rangers in delaying the match, which had been scheduled to take place just three days later. Ibrox chairman David Murray spoke in glowing terms about his Tannadice counterpart as tributes poured in for the United chief.

FRIDAY 16th OCTOBER 2009

Defender Madjid Bougherra landed himself in hot water when he failed to show for training. The Algerian star had been due to return the previous day from international duty, but there was no sign of him as his team-mates prepared to tackle St Johnstone. Bougherra eventually turned up two days late but was dropped from the squad to tackle the Saints as part of the punishment meted out by a frustrated Walter Smith. He had featured in his country's 3-1 World Cup qualifying win against Rwanda the previous weekend.

MONDAY 17th OCTOBER 2011

Concerns that all was not well behind the scenes at Ibrox were compounded when club legend John Greig announced his decision to step down from the Rangers board. He was joined by former chairman John McClelland in making the decision to quit, citing their exclusion from the decision making process under new owner Craig Whyte as the primary reason for their departures. McClelland had been on the board since 2002 while Greig had been appointed as a director a year later.

WEDNESDAY 18th OCTOBER 1961

Harold Davis was renowned as one of the toughest defenders of his generation – but the Rangers hero was a whisker away from becoming an unlikely hat-trick hero as the Ibrox side marked a piece of Hampden history. The club was chosen to play against Eintracht Frankfurt in a match to mark the launch of the national stadium's floodlights. The Germans emerged 3-2 winners, despite the best efforts of Davis as he scored twice and was only denied a treble by the woodwork.

NEWS THAT CLUB LEGEND JOHN GREIG HAD DECIDED TO QUIT THE BOARD AT RANGERS COMPOUNDED FINANCIAL FEARS IN OCTOBER 2011

THURSDAY 19th OCTOBER 2006

Rangers defeated Italian side Livorno 3-2 in the Uefa Cup – but they did it without on-loan Manchester United starlet Phil Bardsley. He had been left out of the travelling party for the game, snubbed by manager Paul Le Guen as punishment for a crunching challenge on Thomas Buffel in training in the build-up to the game. Le Guen said he had to send out a message to the Old Trafford youngster.

TUESDAY 20th OCTOBER 1970

Jim Baxter was back in business after being released by Rangers – but it was not football that he found employment in. The mercurial Ibrox star was granted a pub licence on this day to enable him to take over the Rogano bar on the corner of Paisley Road West and Admiral Street. Slim Jim said he planned to rename the pub Baxter's and was looking forward to forging a new career for himself after calling time on his playing days at the tender age of 31.

MONDAY 21st OCTOBER 1985

The SFA met to consider unsavoury scenes during a Rangers v Aberdeen match at Ibrox and handed out fines of £3000. Two-thirds of that was to be met by the home side, with the Dons picking up the tab for the rest. Craig Paterson and Hugh Burns had both been red carded in the game while coins were thrown from the crowd and fans attempted to climb from the enclosure and make their way towards the pitch during an afternoon of high drama.

THURSDAY 22nd OCTOBER 2009

Hamburg supporters embraced Glasgow's football rivalry when they rolled into the city for their side's Europa League clash with Celtic with Rangers banners and a repertoire of Rangers songs for the occasion. The visitors won 1-0, but it was not without its frustrations for the travelling support as they were denied the opportunity to applaud their heroes at the end of the match due to a police decision to prevent the players from emerging onto the pitch in a bid to prevent further antagonism of the home fans.

WEDNESDAY 23rd OCTOBER 1968

Police launched an investigation at Ibrox after a fire in the early hours swept through the Main Stand, destroying 300 seats. The police interest stemmed from a fire at Hampden just 24 hours previously, but the blazes at two of Glasgow's main football stadiums were said by police to be coincidental.

SUNDAY 23rd OCTOBER 1988

Showdowns with Aberdeen were nothing if not exciting in the late 1980s and the 1988/89 League Cup Final did not disappoint. A pulsating tie at Hampden ended 3-2 in favour of Graeme Souness and his side, but the Dons put up a fight as Davie Dodds twice equalised for the Pittodrie side after Ally McCoist, with a penalty, and Ian Ferguson had scored to put the boys in blue ahead. Souness did not use a single substitute and his decision paid off, with McCoist grabbing his second and Rangers' third.

WEDNESDAY 24th OCTOBER 1956

A bold new era dawned as the club took its place in continental competition for the first time, entered into the European Cup and drawn against French side Nice. The first encounter, fittingly, was at Ibrox and ended in celebration as Scot Symon masterminded a 2-1 victory as Max Murray and Billy Simpson made history with their goals. The second leg ended in a 2-1 defeat, leading to a decider in Paris that saw Nice progress with a 3-1 win.

SATURDAY 24th OCTOBER 1964

It was fitting that Jim Forrest scored both Rangers goals in the 2-1 League Cup Final victory over Celtic. The competition up to that point had Forrest stamped all over it as the young Ibrox starlet made a massive impact. He'd been there at the start of the run, scoring in a 4-0 win against Aberdeen in the opening tie, and went on to net 18 times in ten games – including a four-goal blast against St Johnstone in one group game and a hat-trick against the Perth side in the return fixture. There was also a treble for Forrest against Aberdeen in the group stages.

SATURDAY 24th OCTOBER 1970

A star was born. Derek Johnstone, still cutting his teeth as a first team player, announced his arrival on the big stage when he grabbed the only goal of the League Cup Final to stun Celtic's big name defenders and send the blue half of the 105,263 crowd into raptures. The young Dundonian had made his debut the previous month when he scored a double against Cowdenbeath in the league and helped his side to a 5-2 victory.

SUNDAY 24th OCTOBER 1993

Ally McCoist, in only his fourth game back after recovering from a broken leg, scored a dramatic late winner in the 2-1 League Cup Final victory over Hibs at Celtic Park. It was a perfect time for the talisman to net his first goal of the season, popping up as a substitute to make a major impact. Ian Durrant had also found the net, countering the own goal Dave McPherson had scored to give Hibs hopes of causing an upset.

SUNDAY 25th OCTOBER 1992

Aberdeen must have been sick of the sight of Rangers by the end of the 1992/93 season. They came second best to the Light Blues in all three domestic competitions, with their first attempt at breaking the dominance coming in the League Cup Final at Hampden in October 1992. Stuart McCall's effort and a Gary Smith own goal gave Rangers a 2-1 victory and they went on to get the better of Dons in the Scottish Cup Final and the championship that term.

SUNDAY 25th OCTOBER 1987

Close to 72,000 people were crammed into the old Hampden Park as the national stadium was rocked to its core by a raucous Rangers support during an afternoon of enthralling entertainment as the League Cup was decided on penalties for the first time. It had ended 3-3 after extra time, with Davie Cooper, Ian Durrant and Robert Fleck on target, before the shoot-out commenced. Durrant netted the winning spot kick after Peter Nicholas had clattered the crossbar with his, paving the way for a 5-3 penalty victory.

SATURDAY 25th OCTOBER 1975

It was Alex MacDonald's final as the energetic midfielder popped up with the only goal of a tense League Cup showdown with Celtic. It proved the first trophy in the first treble won by Jock Wallace as Ibrox boss, taking advantage of a kind draw along the way. Queen of the South in the quarter-finals had been nudged aside while Montrose, in the semi-final, were hammered 5-1 by a Gers team firing on all cylinders.

SATURDAY 26th OCTOBER 1963

Hapless Morton were torn apart by wonderkid Jim Forrest at Hampden. Close to 106,000 were inside the national stadium to watch the youth product hit four against the Cappielow men, with Alex Willoughby also on target in a 5-1 victory. The goals in the final brought Forrest's tally to 16 in ten League Cup games that term, including another four in the 5-2 demolition of Queen of the South in the group stages. It was the first trophy in a treble for Scot Symon's side.

SUNDAY 26th OCTOBER 1986

The Graeme Souness revolution was off and running in 1986 when the new manager grabbed his first trophy with a 2-1 win over Celtic at Hampden in the League Cup Final. The player-boss missed the game himself but was there to roar his side on in his first taste of the big occasion as Ibrox chief and they responded with a spirited display. Ian Durrant tucked away the opening goal from close range early in the second half, but Brian McClair equalised. Davie Cooper was the coolest man in the stadium as he stroked home a late penalty to clinch victory.

FRIDAY 27th OCTOBER 2006

Allan McGregor's growing prominence at Ibrox was rewarded with a new three-year contract. The goalkeeper had recorded five clean sheets in eight appearances in the 2006/07 season after stepping in for the injured Lionel Letizi and had pushed himself to the brink of a Scotland place with his impressive displays for the Light Blues. Manager Paul Le Guen said he viewed McGregor as a vital member of staff.

FRIDAY 28th OCTOBER 1983

It was high noon in the Blue Room as chairman Rae Simpson released a short statement to confirm manager John Greig had tendered his resignation, which had been accepted by the board of directors. Earlier that morning he had slipped into Ibrox to bid farewell to his squad after a poor run of form that had led to unrest among sections of the support. Simpson confirmed that Tommy McLean, Greig's assistant, would take charge of the side while the board considered its next move.

SUNDAY 28th OCTOBER 1984

Jock Wallace won his final trophy with Rangers as he guided his struggling Gers side to a tense 1-0 win over Jim McLean's talented and determined Dundee United side. It was former Tannadice player Iain Ferguson who inflicted the knock-out blow, beating veteran Arabs keeper Hamish McAlpine from distance to score the only goal of the game.

SUNDAY 28th OCTOBER 1990

When Graeme Souness got his hands on the League Cup in the autumn of 1990, nobody could have known it would be the last piece of silverware he would land as Rangers manager. The 2-1 win over Celtic at Hampden, when Mark Walters and Richard Gough grabbed the goals, was the early highlight of the season in which he relinquished control and moved south to take charge of Liverpool. The cup final winner proved to be Gough's only goal of the season, but a vital one.

SATURDAY 29th OCTOBER 1960

Rangers and Kilmarnock were nip and tuck all the way to the finish line in the 1960/61 First Division championship race, with the Ibrox side winning the title by a point. Before then the clubs also went head to head in the League Cup Final and again the Ayrshire team hit a brick wall against the dominant Light Blues as Ralph Brand and Alex Scott scored the goals that gave them a 2-0 victory at Hampden. The final proved to be a tougher proposition than the semi-final ten days earlier – when Rangers trounced Queen of the South 7-0 at Celtic Park.

SATURDAY 30th OCTOBER 1965

It was a brave new era for Hamilton as they took their place back at Scottish football's top table for the 1964/65. Their return did not prove to be a happy one as the Accies won just three matches and were relegated, not helped by a 7-1 mauling by Rangers on this day. Jim Forrest was the tormentor-in-chief as he bagged five goals to add to Willie Henderson and Davie Wilson's contributions.

THURSDAY 30th OCTOBER 1986

Scottish clubs went face to face with English rivals for the FA Cup in 1986/87 and a match against Everton on Merseyside was Rangers' introduction to the competition. It ended with success for the Scots, as Charles Heggie scored the only goal of the game. Rangers defeated Church, Glasgow side Cowlairs, Lincoln City and Old Westminsters before falling to a 3-1 defeat against Aston Villa in a semi-final tie played in Crewe.

THURSDAY 31st OCTOBER 1968

Rangers smashed the Scottish transfer record when they agreed to pay Hibs £100,000 to land 21-year-old striker Colin Stein, who became the club and the country's first six-figure player. Everton had been desperate to recruit the bustling frontman but Stein held out to ensure he won his dream move to Ibrox and went on to score a hat-trick on his debut against Arbroath on 2nd November as his new side won 5-1 at Gayfield. He grabbed another treble in his next match, as his old club Hibs were humbled with a 6-1 defeat at Ibrox, and almost made it three in a row when he scored a double in a Fairs Cup tie against Dundalk in his next appearance.

RANGERS
On This Day

NOVEMBER

WEDNESDAY 1st NOVEMBER 1967

Scot Symon, that most loyal of servants, was dismissed just months after leading Rangers to the final of the European Cup Winners' Cup. Symon paid the price for Celtic's success in many ways, ushered out of the door despite bringing silverware to Ibrox during his reign. Just over a fortnight after his departure from the club, the board announced Symon had been appointed an honorary member of Rangers and that they had amicably settled on the terms of his severance. Symon, who had been a star player for Rangers and Scotland, had arrived to take charge after impressing with East Fife and then Preston North End. He had been in charge of Rangers for 13 years when he was asked to clear his desk and move aside for a new man, with his assistant Davie White the candidate chosen to take control

SATURDAY 1st NOVEMBER 1997

Italian star striker Marco Negri made it ten not out when he netted the first of his hat-trick in a 4-1 win against Kilmarnock at Ibrox. It was the tenth consecutive league game in which he had been on the scoresheet, with the incredible run stretching back to the opening day of the season in August. He had already broken the previous top-flight record of scoring in eight matches on the bounce, held by Ally McLeod of Hibs and Frank McDougall of Aberdeen and dating back to the 1970s and 80s, and had scored a phenomenal 23 goals in those ten games. A freak eye injury, suffered during a squash game with team-mate Sergio Porrini, sidelined Negri and ultimately ended his Rangers' career.

SATURDAY 2nd NOVEMBER 1996

Ally McCoist broke the record for post-war top-flight goals when he joined Peter Van Vossen on the scoresheet in a 2-1 win in Kirkcaldy against Raith Rovers. It was Super Ally's 241st Premier Division goal, taking him past the target set by the much travelled former Kilmarnock, Motherwell, Celtic, Hibs and Scotland striker Joe McBride in a career taking in the 1950s, 60s and 70s. The goal was another nail in Raith's coffin as the Stark's Park side slipped towards relegation that season.

WEDNESDAY 3rd NOVEMBER 1971

One of the most dramatic nights in Rangers' long and proud European history took place in Portugal. Having beaten Sporting Lisbon 3-2 in the first leg of the second round of the European Cup Winners' Cup, nobody could have predicted what would unfold in the return match. The 4-3 defeat, in a match that saw defender Ronnie McKinnon suffer a horrific leg break which effectively ended his Ibrox career, left the teams locked at 6-6 on aggregate. The referee famously ordered a penalty shoot-out, which Rangers lost, but journalist John Fairgrieve was on hand with the rule book to point out that away goals counted double and passage to the third round was secured in controversial fashion. The run would end with success in the Barcelona final, but it could have all been so different had it not been for Fairgrieve

WEDNESDAY 4th NOVEMBER 1992

The Battle of Britain took place at Elland Road. At stake was a place in the group stages of the new Champions League and the atmosphere was electric as Rangers travelled south to tackle Leeds United with a 2-1 lead to protect after the 21st October win at Ibrox, when Ally McCoist's effort and an own goal from Leeds keeper John Lukic did the damage to the Yorkshire side's hopes. The decisive tie ended with the same score on the board, with the deadly Hateley and McCoist partnership once again coming up with the goals that mattered at a vital time for Rangers. Leeds, with a glowing reputation on the back of their domestic success, were humbled by their hosts – putting to bed the myth that the Scottish game was significantly worse than that in England and proving that Rangers could compete with the very best.

MONDAY 5th NOVEMBER 1973

Scotland boss Willie Ormond unveiled his squad to face West Germany, with the match against the Germans the following week serving as the focal point of the SFA's centenary celebrations. Rangers would be represented at the gala event by defenders Tom Forsyth and Sandy Jardine, with the big talking point being the recall of striker Peter Lorimer after a two-match international ban.

SATURDAY 6th NOVEMBER 1915

Poor Queen's Park were on the receiving end of another thumping at the hands of Rangers, losing 6-0 at Hampden against a team that had developed a habit of teaching them football lessons. Doubles from Tommy Cairns and Andy Cunningham as well as goals from Jimmy Fleming and Scott Duncan did the damage. Rangers put four past Queen's with almost monotonous regularity in the early part of the century to demonstrate their superiority over their city rivals.

TUESDAY 7th NOVEMBER 1961

A football family welcomed a new addition in Wallasey, near Liverpool. Proud father Tony Hateley was a centre-forward of some repute, starring for Notts County, Aston Villa, Chelsea and Liverpool, and his young son Mark turned out not bad either. Mark Hateley signed for Rangers from Monaco in July 1990 and went on to form one of the most successful striking partnerships the club has ever seen as he and Ally McCoist wreaked havoc throughout the Premier Division during the glory days of the 90s.

SUNDAY 8th NOVEMBER 1998

St Johnstone were on course for one of their most memorable Premier Division seasons, destined to finish third behind the Old Firm. The poor old Saints were brought crashing down to earth by Dick Advocaat and his champions-elect on this day, thumped 7-0 in Perth by a faultless Light Blues side. Jorg Albertz and Stephane Guivarc'h both scored doubles while Rod Wallace, Jonatan Johansson and Andrei Kanchelskis all netted in a ruthless performance.

TUESDAY 9th NOVEMBER 1965

There were 88 minutes on the clock, Scotland had kept the mighty Italians at bay as the two nations went head to head in the World Cup qualifiers. Then it happened. Rangers star John Greig stepped forward to unleash a thunderbolt that rocketed into the net and the Hampden crowd was left delirious – Scotland 1 Italy 0. It was one of the outstanding results for a generation of Tartan Army footsoldiers and provided the Ibrox legend with one of the most memorable goals of his long and distinguished career.

ANDREI KANCHELSKIS NETTED IN A 7-0 THUMPING OF ST JOHNSTONE IN NOVEMBER 1998

THURSDAY 10th NOVEMBER 1983

After protracted talks, it was announced that Jock Wallace was returning to Rangers for a second spell as manager. Motherwell had not been keen to let their boss jump ship but eventually relented when a compensation package, reported to be around £120,000 at the time, was thrashed out. That paved the way for the Gers board to get their man as they sought to replace John Greig, having been rebuffed in approaches for Jim McLean and Alex Ferguson.

MONDAY 10th NOVEMBER 1986

John Paton resigned from his role as chairman. Having held the post since 1983, he cited business reasons for his decision to quit but was making way for David Holmes, who had been serving as chief executive since Lawrence Marlborough had become owner, to take over the top job. Holmes was unlike his predecessors in that he did not hold any shares in the club, having been installed through his role with Marlborough's company the John Lawrence Group, but set about his task with energy and enthusiasm as he worked closely with Souness to broker a string of deals.

SATURDAY 11th NOVEMBER 1972

The changing face of Scottish football became evident as the police got tough with Ibrox fans as Rangers entertained Clyde in a First Division game – following orders from general manager Willie Waddell. He had become concerned about the amount of alcohol consumed on the terraces and urged officers to conduct a purge on carry-outs being taken into the ground by supporters as his bid to keep a close check on behaviour at home matches continued.

FRIDAY 11th NOVEMBER 1983

Hugh Adam became a club director. Adam, who had been a loyal servant and helped to build up the Rangers Pools, was added to the board alongside Tom Dawson and James Robinson as part of a reshuffle in the build-up to Rae Simpson's replacement by John Paton in the chairman's role. The changes came in the wake of Jock Wallace's return as manager as a period of transition on and off the park began.

SUNDAY 11th NOVEMBER 2007

Scottish football's hall of fame had three new Rangers names as Walter Smith, Ally McCoist and legendary defender Eric Caldow accepted their invitation to join the Hampden club. Caldow, with more than 400 Gers appearances to his credit, was there in person to take his place during a glittering ceremony while Brian Laudrup, who himself had been inducted the previous year, was nominated to attend on behalf of Smith and McCoist in their absence.

MONDAY 12th NOVEMBER 1984

Davie Cooper came face to face with some unusual opponents organised by Scotland manager Jock Stein – there were five of them, they were 6ft tall … and they were wooden. The national boss had procured some of the static defensive walls favoured by Italian teams for training as he gathered his squad at Hampden ahead of their crucial World Cup qualifier against Spain. Cooper and Graeme Souness had missed the morning training session, with Souness arriving late after playing commitments in Italy while Cooper had been excused because of a family bereavement.

WEDNESDAY 13th NOVEMBER 1968

Thirteen didn't prove a lucky number for new recruit Colin Stein. Having scored two trebles in his first two games for Rangers after signing from Hibs for £100,000 the striker travelled to Dundalk on Inter-Cities Fairs Cup duty aiming for an unlikely hat-trick of hat-tricks. He came within a whisker of doing that, notching two in a 3-0 win, but bookmakers across the land breathed a sigh of relief when the full-time whistle sounded and his attempt at an odds-defying treble was dashed.

SATURDAY 14th NOVEMBER 1953

Despondent Hamilton won just one of their 30 First Division fixtures in 1953/54 as they plummeted out of the top flight. Any hope they had of adding to their points tally at Ibrox were soon wiped out when the hosts quickly built up an unassailable lead, going on to win 8-1 after being helped in no small way by Willie Thornton's hat-trick. Willie Waddell scored twice while Willie Paton, Johnny Hubbard and Billy Simpson added to the total.

TUESDAY 15th NOVEMBER 1977

John Greig posed with wife Janette and young son Murray outside Buckingham Palace as he travelled to London to be made an MBE following his recognition in the Queen's birthday honours list for his services to football. The Rangers captain was still at the heart of Jock Wallace's team at that stage, not realising it would be his last season as a player. He became the first Rangers star to be honoured by the Royal family.

SUNDAY 15th NOVEMBER 1981

Ibrox stalwart Colin Jackson was honoured with a testimonial match against Everton and more than 25,000 Blue Noses turned out to show their appreciation for the big defender. Jackson, recruited from Aberdeen junior side Sunnybank, had never faltered while wearing the Light Blue shirt but missed his big match through injury. He watched as his team-mates drew 1-1 with the Goodison side, with Derek Johnstone scoring the goal.

SATURDAY 16th NOVEMBER 1929

The bid to equal the club record league win of 10-0 continued in the 1920s and it was Ayr United who were on the receiving end on this date, falling to a 9-0 defeat at Ibrox. Jimmy Fleming scored four on the day while Sandy Archibald and Jimmy Marshall both grabbed doubles and George Brown joined in the fun. It may not have been a record, but it was another two points in the successful run to the First Division championship.

THURSDAY 16th NOVEMBER 1972

European Cup Winners' Cup Final hero Willie Johnston made a sharp exit after his starring role in Barcelona. Just six months after bagging a double in the famous win against Dynamo Moscow, the fiery attacker was sold to West Bromwich Albion for a fee in excess of £100,000. He was in the midst of a 67-day suspension when Baggies boss Don Howe made his move and, after the clubs agreed a fee on 16th November, agreed to make the switch south and follow his fellow Barca Bear Colin Stein to the English game. Stein had earlier been sold to Coventry for £100,000.

SUNDAY 17th NOVEMBER 1968

Rangers offered £50,000 for young St Johnstone midfielder Alex MacDonald. The Perth board met the following evening and, despite interest from Spurs and Sheffield Wednesday, the deal was eventually concluded to take the starlet to his boyhood heroes. MacDonald went on to become a fixture of the Ibrox midfield for a decade and a half, starring in the European Cup Winners' Cup Final in Barcelona in 1972 as well as a string of league and cup victories under Willie Waddell and Jock Wallace.

THURSDAY 18th NOVEMBER 1943

In 1943 Willie Thornton was far from his beloved Ibrox and embroiled in the type of battle that put football in sharp focus. Serving with the Scottish Horse Regiment, Thornton was recognised for his bravery – earning the coveted Military Medal for his gallantry. His heroics came on Sicily as the American and British forces overcame the Germans during a crucial phase of World War II. Thornton, a playing legend thanks to his efforts in Light Blue before and after the war, died in 1991.

FRIDAY 18th NOVEMBER 1983

The shuffle of the coaching pack continued in the wake of John Greig's departure and Jock Wallace's return as manager. It was confirmed that Falkirk boss Alex Totten had agreed to become Wallace's assistant, leading to the departure of existing coaches Tommy McLean and Joe Mason. McLean had been Greig's right hand man while Mason had been in charge of the reserve team. Totten said he was happy to be joining the "greatest club in the world".

SATURDAY 19th NOVEMBER 1960

Rangers were leading by a single goal and edging towards maximum points against Motherwell at Fir Park when the game was controversially abandoned due to fog with just nine minutes left to play. The decision caused something of a stir as the football authorities attempted to determine whether it should be classed as an abandoned or postponed match – and whether it should be replayed. It was eventually contested again, in full, with Rangers gaining justice by winning 2-1.

SATURDAY 20th NOVEMBER 1915

For the first and last time, Rangers started a competitive match with just nine players. Plans for the game at Falkirk in the First Division were hit when John Hempsey, Joe Hendry and Andy Cunningham's travel by train was hit by fog – forcing William Wilton to field a depleted team. Not surprisingly, the Brockville side beat their spirited opponents 2-0 as they took full advantage of their superior numbers to record a victory that stood as far as the league was concerned.

TUESDAY 21st NOVEMBER 1978

The star of Rangers youth product Ally Dawson continued to rise with the young defender called up to Scotland's Under-21 squad for the first time. Dawson, who would go on to captain the club under John Greig, was called up by national team manager Jock Stein along with fellow new face Billy Abercrombie of St Mirren to take his place under coach Eddie Turnbull in the pool for the looming match against Portugal in Lisbon. The Dons boss was to coach the side, although Jock Stein remained in charge of picking the names.

SATURDAY 22nd NOVEMBER 1952

Rangers announced the installation of floodlighting had been completed at Ibrox, paving the way for trials to begin with night time matches. The club went on to arrange a series of matches to test the new pylons. The official launch of the lights came on 8th December 1953 when Arsenal sent a team north and recorded a 2-1 win to spoil the party for their hosts.

TUESDAY 22nd NOVEMBER 1988

Just minutes before midnight in the Ibrox boardroom, pen was put to paper on the deal that transferred control of Rangers Football Club from Lawrence Marlborough to David Murray. The legal formalities were completed just in time, since a delay into the next day would have meant the contracts had to be redrafted to reflect the change in date. On 23rd November Murray was introduced to the nation's press as the new owner of Rangers and the story dominated television and newspaper coverage for days.

THURSDAY 23rd NOVEMBER 2000

A record that could take decades to break was established at Ibrox as Tore Andre Flo put pen to paper on his £12m transfer from Chelsea to Rangers. In a deal that would surely make the accountants wince, the Norwegian striker joined Dick Advocaat's blue revolution. It was second time lucky for the club, having had a bid for the forward rejected in the summer when Advocaat had first arrived.

FRIDAY 23rd NOVEMBER 1984

Never has the recruitment of a 14-year-old schoolboy created the type of headlines that the arrival of John Spencer did on this day. The Eastwood youngster was signed as an S-Form by Jock Wallace and became big news by virtue of the fact he was a Roman Catholic. Chairman John Paton took the opportunity to insist that the club had always stated a Catholic would be signed if the manager deemed the player of suitable ability, with the teenager rejecting approaches from Dundee United and Celtic to commit to the Rangers' cause.

THURSDAY 24th NOVEMBER 2011

Nigerian international winger Sone Aluko became a Rangers player after a deal was struck to pay Aberdeen compensation for their former man. The transfer hit the headlines when Aluko claimed he had dipped into his own bank account to pay the fee, although manager Ally McCoist was quick to play down the part the player had in funding the move. Aluko, who had arrived at the Dons via Birmingham City, proved to be an influential player in the troubled 2011/12 campaign.

SATURDAY 25th NOVEMBER 1893

Cowlairs tackled Rangers at Ibrox in front of 5,000 people in the first round of the Scottish Cup but had no answer to the class of their opponents as they tumbled to an 8-0 defeat, including a hat-trick from Boyd. Leith, another long lost name from the past of the Scottish game, were beaten 2-0 in the second round as Rangers went on a run that ended with them lifting the silverware to enhance the fledgling side's growing reputation as a formidable football force.

SATURDAY 26th NOVEMBER 1988

David Murray took his place in the Ibrox directors' box for the first time and was introduced to the home crowd before the team's match against Aberdeen. He received a rapturous welcome from the Gers faithful and the celebrations continued on the park as Richard Gough popped up with the only goal to get Murray's reign off to a winning start. The crowd of more than 42,000 was the biggest in Britain that day, to give the new major shareholder a taste of what he had bought into.

SUNDAY 26th NOVEMBER 2000

It took 59 minutes for £12m man Tore Andre Flo to get his first goal for the club and he could not have picked a better time to do it. Making his eagerly anticipated entrance in an Old Firm league encounter at Ibrox, the striker knocked home the rebound after a Jorg Albertz header hit the bar to put his side 2-1 ahead. Rangers went on to win 5-1. After Barry Ferguson's opener had been cancelled out by Henrik Larsson and Flo had put the hosts back in front, Ronald de Boer and then Lorenzo Amoruso and Michael Mols had joined the scoring party.

THURSDAY 27th NOVEMBER 1969

It was announced Davie White had been sacked by Rangers. The previous evening his side had crashed out of the European Cup Winners' Cup after a 3-1 defeat at home to Polish side Gornik Zabrze and, amid fierce criticism from some sections of the press and the support, he was relieved of his duties. Dunfermline manager George Farm was installed among the early favourites to replace White as boss at Ibrox.

SATURDAY 28th NOVEMBER 1981

John Greig's final trophy on the frontline for Rangers came in the winter of 1981 when, as manager, he led his troops to the League Cup at Hampden against Jim McLean and his emerging Dundee United side. Davie Cooper and Ian Redford were the scoring heroes, with Redford justifying Greig's decision to invest heavily in him the previous year.

TORE ANDRE FLO TOOK JUST UNDER AN HOUR TO BEGIN PAYING BACK, FOLLOWING HIS ARRIVAL FOR £12m IN NOVEMBER 2000

SATURDAY 28th NOVEMBER 1959

This was the day on which Raith Rovers confirmed they were willing to transfer their young starlet Jim Baxter to Rangers. Rovers boss Bert Herdman confirmed his club was in talks with the Ibrox officials, but stressed no agreement had been reached. In fact, it took another four months for the deal to be struck – with terms agreed in April the following year to pave the way for Baxter's move to Glasgow in a £17,500 deal. Even then, he only linked up with his new side at the end of the 1959/60 campaign.

SUNDAY 29th NOVEMBER 1998

The first trophy is always an ice-breaker for any Old Firm manager and Dick Advocaat got his amid the chill of the winter of 1998 in the League Cup Final at Celtic Park, while Hampden was under renovation. Up to that stage Rangers had breezed through the previous three rounds, scoring 11 and not conceding a single goal in ties against Alloa Athletic, Ayr United and Airdrie. The final was a closer affair, with St Johnstone putting up a fight before falling to a 2-1 defeat. French World Cup winner Stephane Guivarc'h, after just six minutes, and Jorg Albertz, after Nick Dasovic had equalised, were the heroes.

WEDNESDAY 30th NOVEMBER 1960

A club record in Europe was set when German outfit Borussia Monchengladbach were hammered 8-0 in front of an appreciative Ibrox audience in the European Cup Winners' Cup, with the quarter-final match part of the run to the final in that year's competition. Ralph Brand scored a hat-trick, Jimmy Millar grabbed a double and Jim Baxter, Alex Scott and Harold Davis also got in on the act. The first leg had ended 3-0 to Rangers. The record 8-0 victory was not equalled until 14th September 1983 when Maltese side Valetta were beaten by the same margin, with Dave McPherson an unlikely hero with his four goals while Robert Prytz added two and Craig Paterson and John McDonald scored too.

RANGERS
On This Day

DECEMBER

SUNDAY 1st DECEMBER 1985

Jock Wallace and his charges enjoyed some sun on their backs in the 1985/86 season as they escaped to Malta for a two game mini-tour. Having beaten Hamrum Spartans 4-1 on 28th November, the visiting Scots rounded off their trip on 1st December with a resounding 7-0 triumph against Valetta. The standout performer was youngster Scott Nisbet, who had scored twice on his first team debut in the first game and grabbed a hat-trick in the second match to give Wallace food for thought.

MONDAY 2nd DECEMBER 1963

Hopes of winning the British Championship were dashed by Everton, who held their visitors to a 1-1 draw at Goodison Park on this day. The two-legged competition ended with the Merseyside men taking the title by virtue of an impressive 3-1 win at Ibrox, when John Greig's goal was the only consolation.

WEDNESDAY 3rd DECEMBER 2008

Chairman David Murray was awarded an honorary doctorate from Edinburgh University. Murray, educated at Fettes College and Broughton High School in the city, was recognised for his contribution to business and sport. His Edinburgh-based Murray International Holdings employed 3,500 people worldwide by that stage while he was also celebrating 20 years as Rangers owner and had invested heavily in rugby as sponsor of the Scottish national team to give him a foothold in both sports.

FRIDAY 3rd DECEMBER 2010

Craig Whyte met with Rangers chairman Alastair Johnston, having reached an agreement in principle with owner David Murray to buy the club. Whyte and Johnston met in Glasgow, a summit understood to have been organised by Murray as the process began to gather pace. The previous month Whyte had confirmed to the Stock Exchange that he was in talks with a view to purchasing Rangers, having met with Murray and worked towards thrashing out a deal. Johnston became one of the most outspoken critics of Whyte after being ousted in the takeover, although Johnston and some of his board colleagues had voiced concerns even prior to the keys being handed over.

THURSDAY 4th DECEMBER 2008

Scotland may not have been represented at Euro 2008, but Rangers still profited from the tournament. On this day Uefa handed out the compensation to clubs for releasing stars to play in their international showpiece event – albeit it minimally. Bizarrely it was Czech international Libor Sionko who was responsible for the £28,000 bonus winging its way to Ibrox, even though he had left a year earlier. The payout was in recognition of his involvement in his country's qualifiers.

WEDNESDAY 5th DECEMBER 1984

Cardiff City failed in a cheeky bid to land Ally McCoist on loan. Manager Alan Durban, who signed the striker for Sunderland years earlier, noted McCoist's lack of first team opportunities under Jock Wallace and made his move. The Ibrox boss gave the Welsh side short shrift and insisted his striker was not available for a temporary transfer.

TUESDAY 6th DECEMBER 2005

Alex McLeish made history when he became the first manager to guide a Scottish club through to the last 16 of the Champions League. It took a 1-1 draw with Inter Milan at Ibrox to secure Rangers' passage to the knockout stages of the competition, creating a slice of Ibrox history for himself and his team. Peter Lovenkrands was on target to cancel out Adriano's opening goal for the Italians and ease the pressure on McLeish, who had watched his side go ten games without a win and was on the brink of losing his coveted position.

TUESDAY 7th DECEMBER 1971

A trip into the unknown proved a roaring success for Rangers, off the park as much as on it. A game against local opposition in Israel had ended goalless, but the opportunity to train on perfect pitches away from the cold Scottish winter ensured manager Willie Waddell gave the adventure the thumbs-up. Waddell said he was keen to return to the Holy Land after the experiences of the club's first trip to the area. Waddell spoke of being impressed with the facilities and also with the standard of opposition faced by his side.

THURSDAY 8th DECEMBER 1977

The way to a football supporter's heart is through their belly, or so it seemed at the club's annual general meeting in 1977. Among the hot topics of debate were the catering arrangements at Ibrox, with complaints about "wishy-washy" Bovril and a lack of cakes and sandwiches on the matchday menu. Directors defended provisions at the ground and their decision to award the catering contract to an English firm, but did promise to make improvements where possible.

SATURDAY 9th DECEMBER 1899

It was a fond farewell to the first Ibrox Park as Rangers signed off with a 6-1 victory over Kilmarnock. Wilkie scored two, as did Hamilton, while J Robertson and Graham also hit the net. There were 5,000 on hand to witness the historic event as the champions-elect prepared to move to their new home as the club's growth continued apace.

THURSDAY 10th DECEMBER 1970

Glaswegian Alex Cleland was born, not realising the winding path football would take him on. Cleland had been banished to the Dundee United reserves when he was the subject of a shock £750,000 deal that took him and Arabs sidekick Gary Bollan to Ibrox early in 1995. Cleland established himself as a first team regular and was a league, League Cup and Scottish Cup winner with his boyhood heroes. When Walter Smith moved to Everton in 1998 he took Cleland with him. After retiring from playing he went on to carve out a career as a youth coach with Partick, Livingston, Caley Thistle and, most recently, St Johnstone.

TUESDAY 11th DECEMBER 2001

Alex McLeish was welcomed to Ibrox as the new manager of Rangers Football Club, having served his coaching apprenticeship with Motherwell and Hibs. McLeish moved across the country to take charge of a Rangers side being handed over by Dick Advocaat. Chairman David Murray told his new man to ignore speculation that transfer funds would be limited and vowed to continue investing in the squad, with Advocaat remaining on the staff in a director of football role.

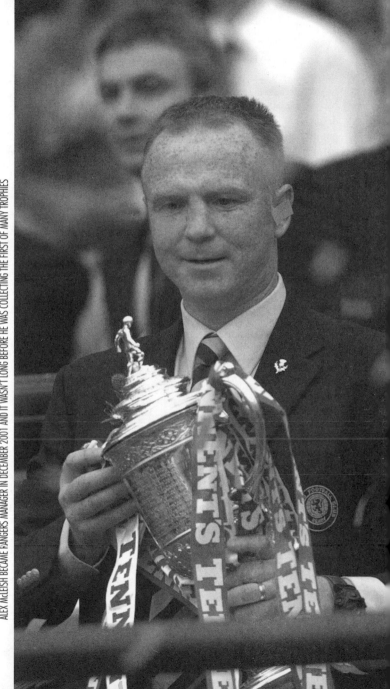

ALEX McLEISH BECAME RANGERS MANAGER IN DECEMBER 2001 AND IT WASN'T LONG BEFORE HE WAS COLLECTING THE FIRST OF MANY TROPHIES

TUESDAY 12th DECEMBER 2006

Rangers were hit with an unusual fine, ordered to pay more than £4,000 after their Uefa Cup tie against Israeli side Maccabi Haifa in November had been interrupted by a lone pro-Palestinian protestor draped in a Palestine flag. Uefa decided the incident merited a hefty punishment and the club opted against appealing the decision.

WEDNESDAY 13th DECEMBER 2000

Rangers officially launched the new electronic swipe cards which would eventually replace the traditional season ticket book. The cards were to be rolled out to 5,000 supporters initially before all 38,000 books were replaced. The scheme represented a £700,000 investment and the club was considering utilising the technology for more than simply gaining entry to the ground, with the potential for individual cards to be used to purchase goods and refreshments at Ibrox. Police were happy with the new development, particularly because it meant cards could be cancelled in an instant if the punishment was deemed appropriate.

THURSDAY 14th DECEMBER 1978

Alex Miller received his reward for playing his part in Rangers' victory over Celtic in the League Cup semi-final the previous evening – a club fine. Miller had been dismissed in a highly charged encounter, along with Celtic's Tommy Burns. Both were hit in the pocket by their clubs, although Miller at least had the consolation of his side's place in the final against Aberdeen after their 3-2 win against Celtic. Rangers won the final 2-1 and Miller appeared from the bench to earn a medal.

SATURDAY 15th DECEMBER 2001

It was out with the old and in with the new as Alex McLeish took charge of Rangers for the first time. His debut as boss ended in a 2-2 draw away to his former club Motherwell, with Neil McCann and Shota Arveladze on target. Bert Konterman and Barry Ferguson were both restored to the team having missed Dick Advocaat's last match, a 1-1 draw at home to Hibs, at the expense of Scott Wilson and Maurice Ross as the era began in less than emphatic style against the struggling Steelmen.

SATURDAY 16th DECEMBER 1899

They didn't know it at the time, but when Rangers defeated St Mirren on this day it was the result that secured the First Division title. It was a home game but one played at Meadowside Park as the transition from old Ibrox to new Ibrox took place. It proved to be a lucky venue as the hosts, in unfamiliar surroundings, triumphed 4-1 against their close rivals with a Hugh Neil double and goals from Alex Smith and Robert Hamilton. When Hearts were defeated by Third Lanark the following week, with Rangers on a day off, the destiny of the prize was secured.

SATURDAY 16th DECEMBER 1967

Rangers were firing on all cylinders as they mounted a challenge for the First Division championship and entertained Raith Rovers on this December afternoon in no mood to show any festive spirit. The ruthless Gers side hammered the Fifers 10-2 as Alex Ferguson grabbed a hat-trick and the trio of Willie Johnston, Orjan Persson and John Greig all claimed doubles. Alex Willoughby was the other goal scorer against Rovers, who were fighting for survival. Rangers would go on to miss out on the league by two points to Celtic while Raith finished one point clear of relegation.

FRIDAY 17th DECEMBER 2010

Defender Madjid Bougherra was the toast of his country, crowned Algerian Footballer of the Year for the second consecutive year. The Ibrox stopper had been a standout performer at both the African Cup of Nations and the World Cup, landing him the recognition from journalists in his homeland.

MONDAY 18th DECEMBER 1961

In the days before penalty shoot-outs in the League Cup, it took two matches to separate Rangers and Hearts when they clashed in the final of the 1961/62 tournament. The first game, on 28th October, finished 1-1 after Jimmy Millar had once again delivered on the big stage. Millar was on target again in the replay along with Ralph Brand and Ian McMillan as west triumphed over east with a 3-1 scoreline against a dogged and determined Jambos outfit.

TUESDAY 19th DECEMBER 1989

English kings Arsenal arrived at Ibrox for a showdown in a match billed as the British Championship, attracting more than 30,000 even at the height of Christmas shopping season. A goal from Mo Johnston gave the home crowd hope, but the visitors claimed the bragging rights with a 2-1 win. Paul Davis had opened the scoring before Mo Jo's equaliser, but Niall Quinn popped up to notch the decisive goal.

MONDAY 20th DECEMBER 1976

There was no festive cheer for the well-drilled Rangers squad as Christmas loomed in 1976. Rather than taking it easy, they were packed off on a bus to travel the road and the miles to Inverness to tackle Clachnacuddin in a friendly on this day. They returned with an 8-0 win under the belts, in time to play Morton at Cappielow in another challenge match the next day. Wallace's men won that one 3-2 to prove they were in fine shape for the New Year programme.

SATURDAY 21st DECEMBER 1929

When Rangers beat Motherwell 4-2 at Ibrox it proved to be a key moment in the 1929/30 First Division campaign. The win, with two goals from Bob McPhail and one apiece from George Brown and Jimmy Fleming, ensured the Steelmen could not make any ground on their opponents and Well eventually ended the campaign in second place, five points adrift of Bill Struth's title-winning charges, at the end of a highly competitive season in which five different sides recorded rare wins against the dominant Light Blues team of the era.

TUESDAY 22nd DECEMBER 1981

The grand unveiling of the redeveloped Ibrox Stadium took place on this day, with Liverpool travelling north to provide the star-studded opposition for the big occasion. The ground was proudly credited with being one of the most modern in world football, with its new predominantly seated design making it a safe and comfortable environment for watching football. The visitors had not made the journey for fun and emerged at the end of the 90 minutes with a 2-1 win.

ONE OF WORLD FOOTBALL'S MOST ICONIC STADIUMS UNDERWENT A MAJOR FACELIFT, WITH LIVERPOOL THE VISITORS TO MARK THE UNVEILING IN DECEMBER 1981

FRIDAY 23rd DECEMBER 2005

Kris Boyd was unveiled as a Rangers player. The striker had cost £450,000 from Kilmarnock and faced a challenge to dislodge Peter Lovenkrands from the main forward's role, with the Dane having netted six goals in four games when Boyd arrived. The Killie man insisted he was ready for the challenge of transferring his impressive Rugby Park scoring form to the big stage of Ibrox. He delivered a hat-trick against Peterhead in the Scottish Cup on his debut.

SATURDAY 24th DECEMBER 1898

Rangers were just a quarter of a century old when they racked up a record that remains to this day. The 10-0 home victory against Hibs was a First Division record for the club and has never been bettered in league competition by generations of Ibrox teams. It was all so easy for William Wilton's men, with Alex Smith scoring four and Hamilton hitting the net twice. There were also goalscoring contributions from McPherson, J Miller, Gibson and Campbell.

THURSDAY 24th DECEMBER 1998

The most protracted transfer of David Murray's tenure as chairman ended on this day as Stefan Klos finally became a Rangers player. The German goalkeeper had first been targeted in the summer of that year but Borussia Dortmund were reluctant to let their man go. It took until the end of the year to secure the £700,000 move for the 27-year-old shot stopper.

SATURDAY 25th DECEMBER 1971

More than 30,000 supporters of Rangers and Hibs opted to give the Queen's Speech a miss and head for Easter Road instead as the two teams tackled each other in the First Division on Christmas Day. The 1971/72 season marked the last time a full set of top-flight games were played on 25th December, ending a tradition stretching back prior to the war. For the record, a Colin Stein goal against his old club proved to be the only goal of the game and gave the Gers fans some festive cheer to take home with them.

FRIDAY 26th DECEMBER 2003

Two new appointments to the Ibrox board were announced – one very familiar name and another that would become well known in the years ahead. The men in question were John Greig, who needed no introduction, and the less well-known Alastair Johnston. As head of global sporting agency IMG, numbering Tiger Woods among his biggest clients, he was a heavyweight appointment and came with the added bonus of a lifelong love of all things Rangers. Johnston would rise to become chairman following his appointment by David Murray.

THURSDAY 27th DECEMBER 2007

Winger Chris Burke vowed to fight for his Ibrox future, despite interest from Colin Hendry's Clyde in taking the youth product to Broadwood on loan. Burke, 24 by then, had struggled to maintain the form that made him one of Scotland's brightest prospects but insisted he had no desire to leave his boyhood heroes.

SUNDAY 28th DECEMBER 1958

Happy birthday Terry Butcher. On this day the former Ibrox and England skipper was born – but it was further from home than his British Bulldog image might suggest. El Tel was born in Singapore, by virtue of his father's role as a signalman in the Royal Navy. Butcher spent the first two years of his life in the country of his birth before returning to English shores and going on to carve out a career in football. Later in life a brief stint as a manager in Australia satisfied the former Ibrox player's emigration curiosity.

THURSDAY 29th DECEMBER 2005

One-time £10m man Francis Jeffers was told his Ibrox dream was over. The former Arsenal starlet had moved north in August on loan from Charlton, with the hope of reigniting his career after a frustrating time following his big money transfer between Everton and the Gunners. The Englishman failed to score a single goal in Rangers' colours, with his chances not helped by niggling injuries, and he was informed there would be no permanent contract on the table. Jeffers returned to Charlton when the transfer window opened in January.

SATURDAY 30th DECEMBER 2006

David Murray was awarded a knighthood in the New Year's honours list. Sir David paid tribute to his family, friends and colleagues as he reacted to the news that he would join the knights of the realm. The recognition for his contribution to business came after more than three decades building his empire, starting with one metal yard in Edinburgh and going on to become head of a global corporation. He was knighted at an investiture in Edinburgh the following summer.

SATURDAY 30th DECEMBER 1995

There's no room for sentiment in football and Gordon Durie proved that when he set about his old team Hibs with vigour. Durie bagged four at Ibrox against the Leith outfit, part of a 7-0 rout against the Hibees. Charlie Miller, Paul Gascoigne and Oleg Salenko joined in to rub salt into the wounds of the visitors. The four-goal blast helped Durie to the Ibrox golden boot, topping the club scoring chart with 17 strikes to Ally McCoist's 16.

SATURDAY 31st DECEMBER 2011

Ally McCoist braced himself for a flurry of activity as he prepared for the January transfer window to open. With interest declared in St Johnstone striker Francisco Sandaza and other targets, the Gers' boss was eager to bolster his squad for the second half of the season and maintain a title challenge. The window turned out to be a damp squib, not helped by the loss of Nikica Jelavic to Everton, as it became apparent the club's financial struggles were having an impact on McCoist's team-building plans. The slide towards liquidation was underway.